TALKABOUT
for
CHILDREN

DEVELOPING SOCIAL SKILLS

ALEX KELLY

www.speechmark.net

Published by
Speechmark Publishing Ltd, 70 Alston Drive, Bradwell Abbey, Milton Keynes
MK13 9HG, United Kingdom
Tel: +44 (0) 1908 326944 Fax: +44 (0) 1908 326960
www.speechmark.net

002-5746/Printed in the United Kingdom by CMP (uk) Limited

British Library Cataloguing in Publication Data
A catalogue record for this book is available from the British Library.

ISBN 978 0 86388 869 4

Contents   Page

iii

TALKABOUT for CHILDREN

Acknowledgements

I would like to thank the following people for their support in writing this book:

Jenny Savage – thank you for your imagination, endless ideas and practical help. Gary and Brad owe a lot to you!

Amy Wright-Green – thank you for your continued enthusiasm and support and endless testing of games with the inevitable laminating and colouring in!

Brian Sains – thank you for your never ending support in everything, including writing this book. Thank you especially for the animals – they are down to you! And thank you also for being the loveliest person in my life!

I would really like to thank everyone who has attended one of my training or lecturing events and given me such positive feedback on my ideas and resources. I love the fact that I am able to share my enthusiasm and passion for this subject, but the feedback I receive from everyone makes my job so much lovelier!

I would like to thank the following people for piloting this resource and for giving me feedback: Elizabeth Blutman, Deborah Goodfellow, Rachel Hughes, Sandra McGlynn, Sam Malpass, Sarah Newhouse, Sarah Sharpless and Sharon Smith. I would also like to thank the following schools for piloting the TALKABOUT resources over the past year and allowing me to assess the effectiveness of this approach: Northcott School in Hull, Redwood Park School in Portsmouth, Brookfields School in Reading, Forest Park School in Totton and Oak Lodge School in Hythe.

I would also like to thank the Alex Kelly Ltd speech and language therapy team for their hard work and enthusiasm: Naomi Carter, Sean Douglas, Kathleen Hanson and Amy Wright-Green.

Finally I would like to thank my children - Ed, Peter and George who regularly have to put up with a mum who is busy, away from home or distracted. Thank you for your love and support and also for your help with some of these activities!

This book is dedicated to my mum and dad – thank you for always being there for me and for everything you do to make my world special.

About the author

Alex Kelly is a Speech and Language Therapist with 25 years experience of working with both children and adults with a learning disability, and specialising in working with children who have difficulties with social skills, self esteem and relationship skills. She runs her own business (Alex Kelly Ltd) providing training and consultancy work to schools and organisations in social skills around the UK and abroad. She also currently employs 4 speech and language therapists and provides speech and language therapy at 6 special schools in Hampshire. She is the author of the best selling 'Talkabout' resources.

Introduction

An overview of this book

TALKABOUT for Children is a practical resource to help teachers or therapists to develop social skills in children. It has been particularly aimed at primary school children (aged 4–11) or children with special needs (aged 5–16).

TALKABOUT for Children: developing social skills is a stand-alone resource with 2 years' worth of activities to develop social skills. It has over 60 activities to make up and play with children and it has been successfully piloted in the UK and Australia.

It is the second book of 3 resources aimed specially at younger children or children with special needs:

1. TALKABOUT for Children: developing self awareness and self esteem
2. TALKABOUT for Children: developing social skills
3. TALKABOUT for Children: developing friendships (due in 2012).

TALKABOUT for Children: developing social skills is a complete practical resource which includes:

- An assessment of a child's social skills

- 60 activities to play to develop social skills

- Practical suggestions to make your group work successful including 25 group cohesion activities, a plan for intervention, and forms for monitoring and evaluation.

This resource continues to use the TALKABOUT hierarchical approach to teaching skills. This means that basic skills are taught first and more complex skills last. So that if a child needs social skills work in all the

3

areas assessed, the resource should be used logically from level 1 through to level 3.

Following this, if children also have friendship skills difficulties, they could then progress onto the third TALKABOUT for Children book – developing friendship skills.

TALKABOUT for Children includes an assessment, 3 sections to teach social skills, a section on group cohesion activities and finally a section on planning your intervention which includes practical suggestions to make your group successful.

1. TALKABOUT Social skills assessment

This is your initial assessment of social skills which assesses a child's body language, the way they talk, conversational skills and assertiveness skills using a 4 point rating scale. These results are then summarised on the assessment wheel and a plan of intervention is agreed.

2. TALKABOUT Body Language

This level aims to increase children's awareness and use of body language. It is divided into 4 topics:
1. Talking body language
2. Talking faces
3. Talking bodies
4. Talking space.

3. TALKABOUT Talking

This level aims to increase children's awareness and use of speaking and listening skills in conversations. It is divided into 6 topics:
1. Talkabout talking
2. Talkabout speaking
3. Talkabout listening
4. Talkabout beginnings

4

5. Talkabout taking turns
6. Talkabout endings.

4. TALKABOUT Assertiveness

This level aims to increase the children's awareness and use of assertiveness skills. It is divided into 6 topics:

1. Saying something
2. Saying what I think
3. Saying how I feel
4. Saying no
5. Saying sorry
6. Saying something nice.

5. GROUP COHESION ACTIVITIES

This section includes 25 of my favourite group cohesion activities.

6. PLANNING your intervention

This section includes suggestions for making your group work successful, including:

1. A plan of intervention for each area of social skills
2. Forms for evaluation and planning
3. Certificates of attendance.

Developing social skills – using the hierarchical approach

The importance of being socially skilled cannot be over estimated. We all need these skills to communicate effectively in order to listen to others, to express ourselves, to be taken seriously, to learn and to make friends. And we know that social competence contributes to quality of life and has been repeatedly demonstrated to be a critical variable in predicting success in future life. However not all children develop social competence naturally. Some children are socially unskilled and require intervention. So

what can be done to help them? Where do you start and how can it be done?

Choosing the right place to start work has to be the most important part of intervention as it is the difference between potentially setting a child up to fail or succeed.

Results from social skills work in the early nineties led to the development of a hierarchy which is the basis of the 'Talkabout' resources. It was found that the success of intervention increased if non verbal behaviours were taught prior to verbal behaviours, and assertiveness was taught last. For example, children working on their verbal or conversational skills progressed more if they already had good non verbal skills, and children working on their assertiveness progressed significantly more if they had existing good non verbal and verbal skills. In addition, it was found that a basic self and other awareness was important to teach as a pre-requisite to social skills training. A hierarchy was therefore proposed, piloted and found to be highly successful.

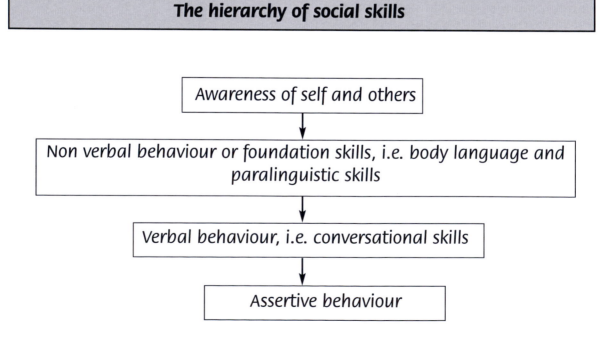

| The hierarchy of social skills |

Awareness of self and others

↓

Non verbal behaviour or foundation skills, i.e. body language and paralinguistic skills

↓

Verbal behaviour, i.e. conversational skills

↓

Assertive behaviour

This is logical. Think about conversational skills; they are more complex than the non verbal behaviours. For example, consider listening: a good listener uses appropriate eye contact and facial expression to show they are listening. Now consider turn taking: this needs good listening which in turn needs eye contact etc. So choosing the wrong skill to start work on, i.e. a skill that is too complex will potentially set a child up to fail.

Using this hierarchical approach, teachers are able to start work with the children at a level that is appropriate to their needs and progress up the levels to enable them to reach their full potential. This hierarchical approach forms the basis of all the Talkabout resources.

Setting up a TALKABOUT social skills group

Group membership

It is important to match the children in terms of their needs and also how well they are going to get on. A group is far more likely to gel and work well if they have similar needs, are a similar age and like each other. Group membership should also be closed, i.e. you should not allow new members to join half way through, as this will alter the group dynamics. I often work with peer groups, i.e. children from the same class or year, but it may be more appropriate to choose children from several year groups and classes. If this is the case, I try to have children who are no more than 2 years apart in age.

The size of the group

Groups work best if they are not too small or too big, preferably between 4 and 8. I usually aim for a group of 6. You need them to be small enough to make sure that everyone contributes and feels part of the group and large enough to make activities such as role plays and group discussions feasible and interesting. Even numbers are helpful if you are going to ask them to sometimes work in pairs. When I am asked to work with whole

classes, I usually manage this by dividing the class into smaller groups and trying to find a spare classroom to use. Sometimes it is good to come back together at the end of the lesson to share one thing from each group. This does take longer though so you need to allow an extra 5 minutes for this.

Length of the sessions

Timings are given at the beginning of each topic but it is important to remember that change will not happen quickly. You should really allow at least a whole academic year (39 weeks) to be able to work through all these activities. In terms of the sessions, it is important that you have enough time to get through your session plan (see next section) but not so much time that the children get bored. I usually aim for about 40 minutes.

Group leaders

Groups run better with two leaders, especially as there is often a need to model behaviours, observe the children, work video cameras and facilitate group discussions. Running groups on your own is tiring and often unsatisfactory. It is also important to remember that when working on self esteem, children may choose to share things that need you to act and another adult in the room is very helpful.

Accommodation

You will need a room that is comfortable for the children to learn in, where you are not going to be interrupted. Don't be tempted to accept the corner of the hall or library as an acceptable place to run your group – this will not help your children to relax and talk openly. In terms of the layout of chairs, I sometimes work around a table depending on the activity; however, it is usually helpful to start with the chairs in a circle for the group cohesion activity.

Parental permission

Remember to get parental permission for the children to join the group and also to be recorded if video cameras are going to be used within the sessions.

Support from management

It is always helpful to have support from management. You may need to outline the objectives, benefits and requirements of the group before you start so that you refer back to them if necessary.

Running the group

Cohesiveness

A group that does not gel will not learn or have fun. It is therefore important to take time to ensure that group gelling occurs. Things that help are:

- interpersonal attraction – children who like one another are more likely to gel

- similar needs

- activities that encourage everyone to take part and have fun

- arranging the chairs into a circle prior to the session

- ensuring that everyone feels valued in the group

- ensuring that everyone feels part of the group and has an equal 'say'

- asking the group to set some rules

- starting each session with a relatively simple activity that is fun and stress free

- finishing each session with another activity that is fun and stress free.

See the group cohesion section for my favourite 25 group cohesion activities.

The format of the session

The format of the session will vary from time to time but there are general guidelines which should be followed:

Group cohesion activity This brings the group together and helps them to focus on the purpose of the group. The activity should be simple, stress free and involve everyone.

Main activity It is during this part of the session that it is most important not to lose children's interest or attention by allowing an activity to go on for too long, or one child to dominate the conversation.

Finishing activity A group activity to reduce any anxiety and to help the children leave in a happy and positive frame of mind. It should therefore be fun, simple and stress free.

In addition, you could also use the following activities from the first TALKABOUT for Children book every week:

How am I feeling? This activity encourages children to explore and discuss their feelings using a simple feeling board. I would do this after the first group cohesion activity.

How did I do? I usually ask the children to think about how they found the session using a familiar traffic light rating scale: green = I did well or that was good; amber = I did OK or that was OK; red = I found that hard. I usually do this before the last group cohesion activity.

My record of achievement I sometimes reward the children for their behaviour in the group by allowing them to choose a sticker as they leave and to place it on their record of achievement. I then laminate this later as a certificate. A template for this can be found in the first TALKABOUT for Children book.

Confidentiality

It is important to remind the children not to talk about what other children have shared with the group outside of the session.

Have fun!

Children learn much more readily if they are having fun. It is important to work hard to make sure the children want to come to the sessions and a large part of this motivation will come from whether they enjoy them.

Transference of skills

It is essential that any work that is being done within the group is backed up outside of the group. I would encourage you to get other staff on board so that they can be aware of what you are doing with the children. Look for opportunities for children to receive praise or positive feedback within their everyday environment and identify any parts of their day that are not conducive and deal with them. You should also try to involve families where it is appropriate to do so, so that skills are reinforced at home.

See CD for all relevant activity pages

This symbol *appears* where all pages relevant to this activity are available on the CD that accompanies the book

 Introduction to Assessment

Objectives   To provide a baseline assessment

To plan where to start intervention

Materials   1. Social skills assessment

2. Planning intervention sheet

Timing   The timing of the assessment will depend on how well you know the child. If you do not know the child well, then you will need to talk to a number of people for their opinions on the child's social skills. If you know the child well, then the assessment should only take 20 minutes.

ASSESSMENT

Introduction to Assessment

Activity	Teacher notes
Social skills assessment	This is a full assessment of the child's social skills. Complete the assessment using a consensus of opinions from other people who know the child well. You can involve the child in the process if appropriate, i.e. if the child is able to understand the activity. Transfer the assessment to the assessment summary pie chart. This assessment is also available to buy on CD rom.
Planning intervention	Use the information from the 1:1 interview and social skills assessment to plan where to start, using the hierarchy.

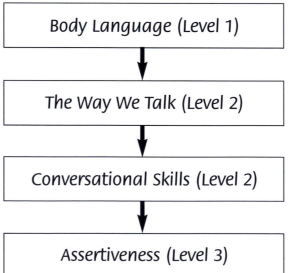

Body Language (Level 1)

↓

The Way We Talk (Level 2)

↓

Conversational Skills (Level 2)

↓

Assertiveness (Level 3)

⊛ Social Skills Assessment

Name.. DOB...........................

Class.. Date...........................

1	2	3	4
Never Good	**Not Very Good**	**Quite Good**	**Very Good**
☹	☹	☺	☺

Complete the assessment using a consensus of opinions from other people who know the child well.

Involve the child in the process if appropriate.

Transfer the assessment to the assessment

Body Language

	1	2	3	4	
Eye Contact Never Good - avoids eye contact at all times during conversations or continuously stares	☹	☹	☺	☺	Very good - effective and appropriate use of eye contact in all situations
Facial Expression Never Good - inappropriate to situation. May include scowling, grinning, blank expression etc.	☹	☹	☺	☺	Very good - effective use of a range of facial expressions, changing according to the situation, e.g. expresses own moods and feelings through facial expressions
Gestures Never Good - uses inappropriate hand gestures excessively, or no use of hand gestures	☹	☹	☺	☺	Very good - uses hand gestures effectively, e.g. for emphasis or substitution of speech
Distance Never Good - inappropriate distance when communicating causing discomfort to others	☹	☹	☺	☺	Very good - adapts distance appropriately and effectively, i.e. according to relationships and social situations
Touch Never Good - excessive use or avoidance of touch which causes embarrassment or anger in others	☹	☹	☺	☺	Very good - effective and appropriate use of touch, i.e. a degree of touch which is acceptable to others and/or the situation
Fidgeting Never Good - excessive fidgeting that is distracting and causes a barrier to communication	☹	☹	☺	☺	Very good - rarely fidgets
Posture Never Good - usually inappropriate to situation, e.g. inappropriately rigid or relaxed	☹	☹	☺	☺	Very good - normal posture and gait, appropriate to all situations
Personal Appearance Never Good - habitually unkempt appearance and/or inappropriate clothing to season or situation	☹	☹	☺	☺	Very good - maintains and adapts appearance to different situations, seasons and age. Uses appearance to create different impressions

15

ASSESSMENT

The Way We Talk

	1	2	3	4	
Volume Never Good - Mostly uses inappropriate volume, e.g. voice too loud or quiet for the situation	☹	☹	☺	☺	Very good - uses and adapts volume appropriately in all situations
Rate Never Good - consistently inappropriate rate, e.g. too fast, slow, fluctuating between two extremes	☹	☹	☺	☺	Very good - rate of speech is appropriate and adapted effectively, e.g. increasing rate when there is a sense of urgency
Clarity Never Good - habitual use of indistinct speech, e.g. mumbling	☹	☹	☺	☺	Very good - speech is consistently clear and easily understood
Intonation Never Good - consistently inappropriate, e.g. monotonous or exaggerated	☹	☹	☺	☺	Very good - intonation is used effectively and appropriately, i.e. adapted to situation and content of speech
Fluency Never Good - consistently dysfluent, e.g. severe hesitations in speech, excessive use of 'um' and 'er'	☹	☹	☺	☺	Very good - fluent speech

Conversational Skills

	1	2	3	4	
Listening Never Good - difficulty in listening and lack of non verbal reinforcement, e.g. eye contact, nodding	☹	☹	☺	☺	Very good - a good listener showing effective and appropriate use of non verbal reinforces
Starting a Conversation Never Good - rarely initiates a conversation or inappropriate to situation, e.g. habitual subject matter	☹	☹	☺	☺	Very good - effective and appropriate use of conversation starters
Taking Turns Never Good - monopolises conversations with minimal listening or makes few contributions	☹	☹	☺	☺	Very good - uses good turn taking skills and effectively responds to cues, e.g. natural breaks, eye contact, questioning
Asking Questions Never Good - does not ask questions during conversations or seek further information when needed	☹	☹	☺	☺	Very good - asks questions with appropriate frequency especially when gaining information to maintain a conversation
Answering Questions Never Good - does not answer questions during conversations or uses minimal utterances, e.g. yes, no	☹	☹	☺	☺	Very good - responds to questions effectively and appropriately to maintain a conversation
Being Relevant Never Good - has difficulty in following a topic of conversation, e.g. introduces unrelated ideas	☹	☹	☺	☺	Very good - can maintain and develop a topic effectively and appropriately
Repairing Never Good - does not seek clarification or further information when a misunderstanding occurs	☹	☹	☺	☺	Very good - seeks clarification and further information effectively and appropriately
Ending a Conversation Never Good - has great difficulty in ending conversations or walks off without adequate closure	☹	☹	☺	☺	Very good - consistently ends conversations effectively and appropriately with appropriate non verbal and verbal behaviour

16

Assertiveness

	1	2	3	4	
Expressing Feelings *Never Good - does not express feelings or needs effectively or appropriately. May appear passive or aggressive in their ability to tell you*	☹	☹	☺	☺	*Very good - effective and appropriate expression of feelings or needs, i.e. expresses feelings with appropriate body language and vocabulary*
Standing Up For Yourself *Never Good - does not stand up for self or rights and may appear passive or aggressive or will stand up for self inappropriately*	☹	☹	☺	☺	*Very good - stands up for self or rights effectively and appropriately, i.e. can represent own views and feelings in an assertive way*
Making Suggestions *Never Good - does not make suggestions, may appear passive, easily led; or continuously making suggestions, not listening to others*	☹	☹	☹	☺	*Very good - makes suggestions or gives opinions effectively and appropriately and in the correct context*
Refusing *Never Good - will always comply with requests even when against their will or will refuse aggressively, inappropriately or continuously*	☹	☹	☺	☺	*Very good - intonation is used effectively and appropriately, i.e. adapted to situation and content of speech*
Disagreeing *Never Good - does not disagree with opinions and may appear passive or easily influenced or will disagree aggressively or continuously*	☹	☹	☺	☺	*Very good - has well developed skills in refusal which are used effectively and appropriately, i.e. uses appropriate non verbal and verbal behaviour*
Complaining *Never Good - does not complain when appropriate or may communicate dissatisfaction inappropriately and complain continuously*	☹	☹	☺	☺	*Very good - complains effectively and appropriately to the situation by stating reasons clearly and assertively*
Apologising *Never Good - does not apologise when appropriate or expected, may be defensive or aggressive or continuously apologises inappropriately*	☹	☹	☺	☺	*Very good - apologises effectively and appropriately using appropriate verbal and non verbal behaviour*
Requesting Explanations *Never Good - does not question requests or decisions and may respond inappropriately to them or continuously requests inappropriately*	☹	☺	☺	☺	*Very good - shows effective skills in requesting further explanations when necessary*

Comments

Completed by .... Date ....

ASSESSMENT

👤 Social Skills Assessment Summary

Name ....

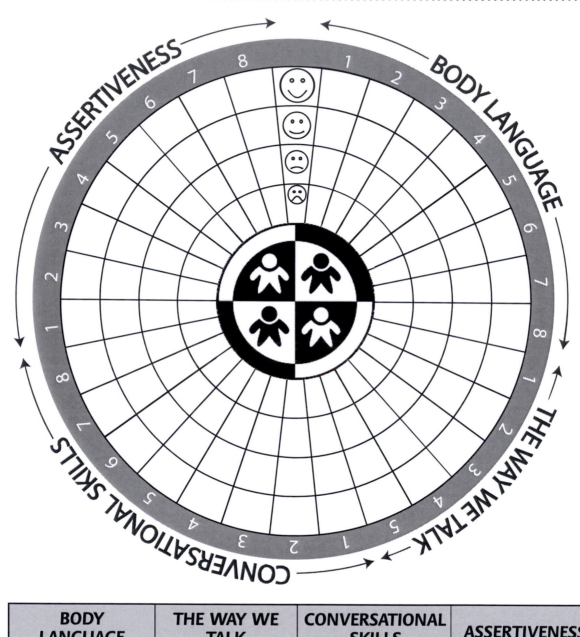

BODY LANGUAGE	THE WAY WE TALK	CONVERSATIONAL SKILLS	ASSERTIVENESS
1. Eye contact	1. Volume	1. Listening	1. Expressing feelings
2. Facial expression	2. Rate	2. Starting a conversation	2. Standing up for yourself
3. Gestures	3. Clarity	3. Taking turns	3. Making suggestions
4. Distance	4. Intonation	4. Asking questions	4. Refusing
5. Touch	5. Fluency	5. Answering questions	5. Disagreeing
6. Fidgeting		6. Being relevant	6. Complaining
7. Posture		7. Repairing	7. Apologising
8. Personal appearance		8. Ending a conversation	8. Requesting explanations

18

Planning Intervention

Name.. DOB...........................

Class... Date...........................

Social skills	Needs work?	Start here

Body Language...
Refer to social skills assessment

NO   YES →

Level 1
Talkabout Body Language

The Way We Talk...
Refer to social skills assessment

NO   YES →

Level 2
(Topics 1 & 2)
Talkabout Talking

Conversational Skills...
Refer to social skills assessment

NO   YES →

Level 2
(Topics 1, 3-6)
Talkabout Talking

Assertiveness Skills...
Refer to social skills assessment

NO   YES →

Level 3
Talkabout Assertiveness

Additional Comments

Completed by .... Date ....

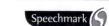

Contents

*C/V = colour version of worksheet available on the CD

Introduction

Aim of this level	To increase awareness of body language and to improve skills in using body language effectively.
Topics covered	1. Talking body language 2. Talking faces 3. Talking bodies 4. Talking space.
Length of level	This level will take up to 24 lessons depending on the ability of the students and the length of the lessons.
Students	Groups work best if the children get on and are well matched for both personality and need. Aim for a group of between 4 and 8 people. Remember that a larger group will mean the level may take longer to complete.
Group gelling	Factors that can help group cohesion are: group cohesion activities (see pages 247–48); getting the group to decide on a name for the group; devising some group rules; making sure everyone takes part; and good leadership.
Format of the sessions	1. Group cohesion activity 2. Recap 3. Main activity(s) 4. Group cohesion activity.
Confidentiality	Remind everyone that the content of the sessions is not to be discussed with other students outside of the session.

Topic 1: Talking body language

Objectives: To introduce the concept of body language

To gel the group

To introduce the 3 key areas of face, body and space

Materials: You will need to print out and copy a number of the activities

Some of the activities are best enlarged to A3

Some of the activities are best laminated so that you can use them again

You may need a bean bag for one activity

Timing: This topic will take up to 4 sessions to complete.

Topic 1: Talking body language

Activity	Teacher notes
Silent movies (Activity 1)	A team game to explore how we can communicate without the use of words. An exercise to introduce the areas of our face; our body and the use of space.
Building bodies (Activity 2)	The children create a man from body parts and discuss which parts of our body can be used to communicate. These are then coloured in on a worksheet.
Dissecting bodies (Activity 3)	The children identify all the different ways that they used their body to communicate certain emotions and actions in activity 1.
Talking body parts (Activity 4)	The children choose a card with a body part on it and they have to use that part of their body to communicate something.
Our Talkabout rules (Activity 5)	A poster is prepared for the children to refer to for the rest of the level.

Activity 1: Silent movies

Preparation

Print out the 6 cards. Each scenario has a few prompts for the facilitators to use if necessary. These can be printed off and made up back to back.

Laminate the cards if you wish to use them again.

You will also need a camera to take photos of the children.

Instructions

- Ask the children to get into 2 teams.

- Each team is given a scenario to act. They are both given a few minutes to prepare their mime. They need to think about who is going to act it out (anything from 1 person to the whole team) and what they are going to do.

- It is helpful to have 1 facilitator per team and they can help the children plan their mime by using the prompts.

- Each team performs their mime and the other team tries to guess what is on their card.

- Photos are taken at key moments to illustrate different aspects of body language (to be used in Activity 3).

Activity 1: Silent movies

I am really bored. I hate this lesson and I wish it was lunch time as I am getting hungry.
 	
(1 actor or more)
	PROMPTS
	
	FACE: *eyes to clock*
	         eyes looking up
	         face looks bored or blank
	         lips together
	
	BODY: *posture slouched*
	         fidgeting
	
	SPACE: *n/a*

It's my birthday today and my friend has just given me a really great present. I am so happy!
 	
(2 actors or more)
	PROMPTS
	
	FACE: *eyes wide*
	         eyes looking at friend
	         face looks happy
	         lips apart
	
	BODY: *posture relaxed*
	         lots of gesture
	
	SPACE: *hugging friend*

I am very worried. My cat has not come in for his supper. I have tried calling him but he is nowhere to be seen.
 	
(1 actor or more)
	PROMPTS
	
	FACE: *eyes looking around*
	         eyes narrowed
	         face looks worried or sad
	         forehead frowning
	
	BODY: *posture slightly tense*
	         hands to mouth / chin
	
	SPACE: *n/a*

Activity 1: Silent movies

I am really upset. Someone has just called me a horrible name. My friend is being very kind to me and trying to make me feel better

(3 actors or more)

PROMPTS

FACE: eyes downward & narrow
face looks sad
lips together

BODY: posture slouched
hands to face

SPACE: friend comforts using touch
hugging

I am very angry. The teacher has just told me off for something the person sitting next to me did.

(3 actors or more)

PROMPTS

FACE: eyes wide
looking at teacher & friend
face looks angry

BODY: posture tense
lots of gesture

SPACE: gets close to friend in threatening way

I am very scared. We have just watched a very frightening film and I am now frightened to go to bed.

(2 actors or more)

PROMPTS

FACE: eyes wide
looking around
face looks very worried
forehead frowning

BODY: posture tense
hands to mouth / chin

SPACE: gets close to other person

Activity 2: Building bodies

Preparation

Choose whether you want to use colour or black and white body parts.

Print out the body and the body parts. If possible enlarge both to A3 or redraw the body onto a large piece of flip chart or sugar paper.

Cut out the body parts and laminate if you wish to use them again. This will also make them easier to handle.

You will also need a 'feely' bag or something to put the body parts in. Print out the worksheets.

Instructions

- Put the main body in the middle of the circle.

- Take it in turns to remove a body part from the feely bag.

- Ask the child to put it on the body and to say whether they think that part of our body can be used for communication. Some of their answers will depend on the level of the children. For example, items such as hair or jewellery can be used to communicate individuality and feelings, but this is a higher level concept, so for younger children you may agree that we don't communicate though our hair or accessories.

- Children then decorate their own body on their worksheet and colour in or identify the parts that can be used for communication.

Activity 2: Building bodies

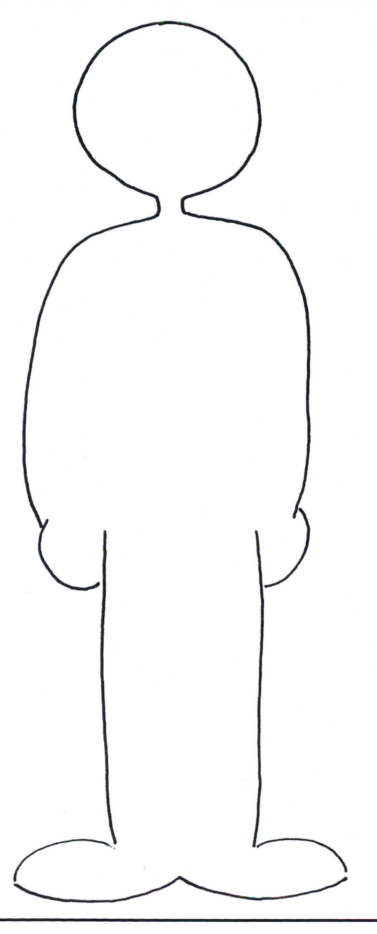

👤 Activity 2: Building bodies

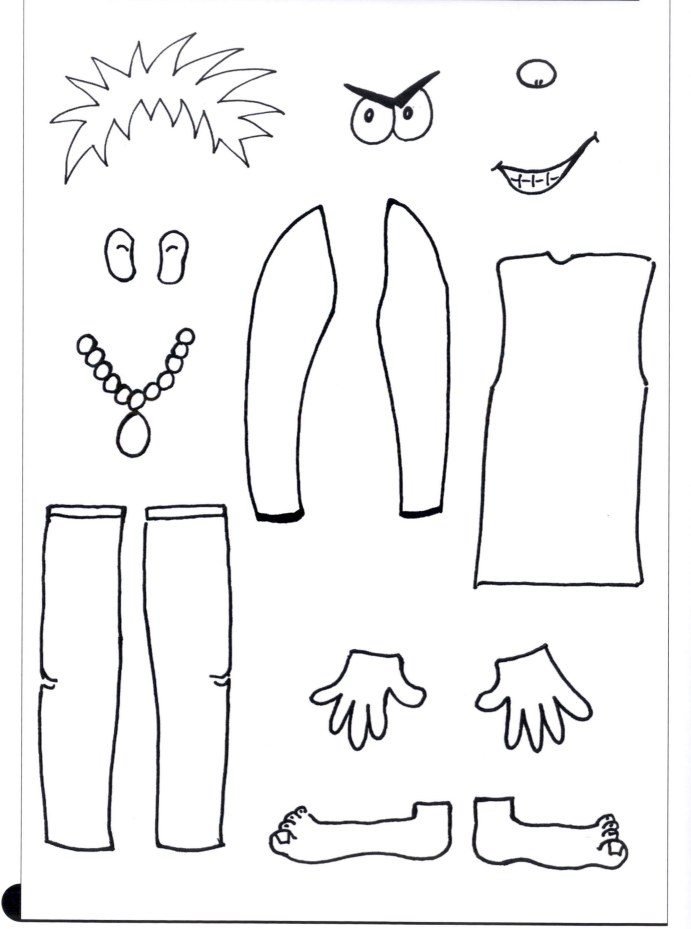

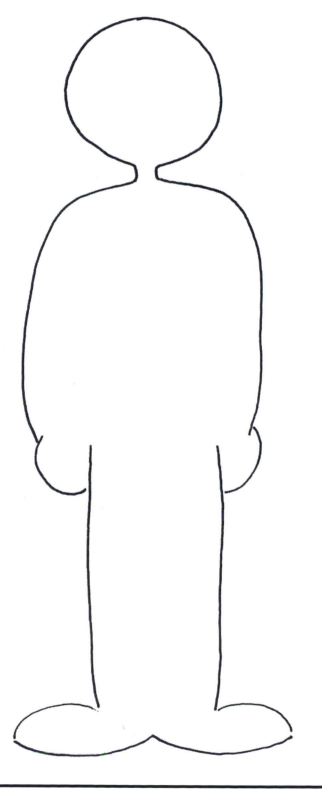

Activity 2: Building bodies   Worksheet

Name _____ Date _____

Which parts of our body do we communicate with? Can you identify them? You could add hair, eyes and clothes if you want.

 **Activity 3: Dissecting bodies**

Preparation

Choose whether you want to use colour or black and white worksheets and print out enough for each photo you want to analyse. These are best done larger than A4, so if possible, enlarge the main worksheet to A3.

Choose which photos you are going to use from Activity 1. Try to choose a range of emotions: angry, happy, scared, worried etc. You will need one set of worksheets for each photo.

You will also need scissors and glue.

Instructions

- Choose 1 photo to start with and stick in the middle of the worksheet.

- Ask the children to try and notice what is happening to their body.

- Use the pictures on the second worksheet to think about their face, eyes, posture, hands and distance / touch.

- The children then cut and stick the appropriate pictures onto the worksheet.

- They then move on to another photo and worksheet.

- If you are unable to use photos from Activity 1, use photos of people from the internet expressing the same emotions and ask the children to remember how they acted that particular emotion.

Activity 3: Dissecting bodies　　　Worksheet

Name_____ Date _____

This person is feeling .... **How can we tell?**

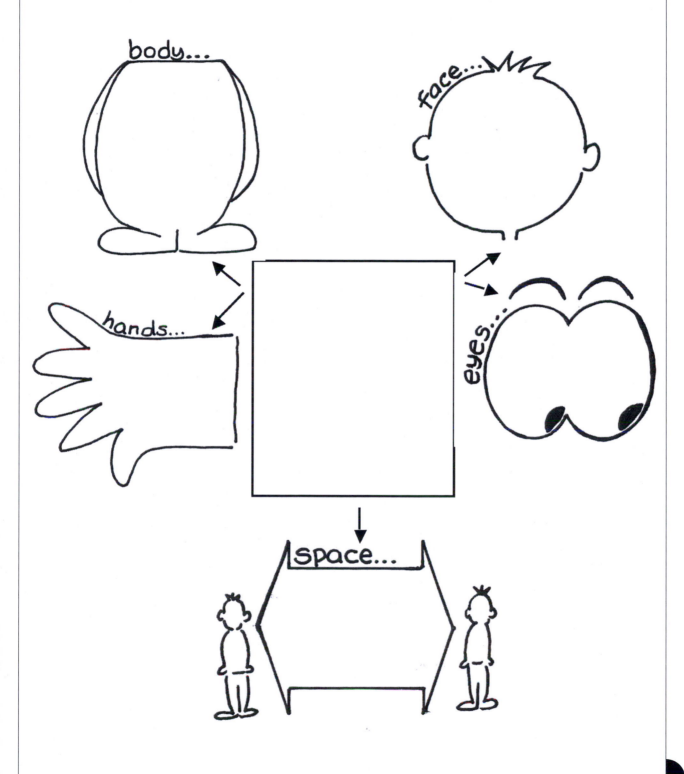

 Activity 3: Dissecting bodies

face...

 **Happy**	 **Sad**	 **Worried**	 **Angry**
 **Bored**	 **Scared 1**	 **Scared 2**	 **Good looking**

eyes...

 **Eyes wide**	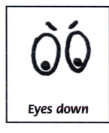 **Eyes raised**	 **Eyes down**	**Eyes moving around**

body...

 **Tense**	 **Relaxed**	 **Slouched**	 **Good posture**

hands...

 **Clenched fist**	 **Fidgety hands**	 **Hands to mouth/face**	**Hands relaxed**

space...

 **Hugging**	 **Touch**	 **Gets close to someone**

34

Activity 4: Talking body parts

Preparation

Choose whether you want to use colour or black and white cards and print out. You may choose to enlarge the cards and place them on a large coloured mat (you may have already made one of these – see TALKABOUT for Children: developing self awareness, activities 2 and 29). You will then also need a bean bag and Velcro to attach the cards to the mat.

Instructions

- Explain to the children that they are going to act using different parts of their bodies.

- There are 8 different cards and the children take it in turns to select a card either by picking one or throwing a bean bag onto the mat.

- They then need to use that part of their body to communicate something – either an emotion or an activity.

- Can the others guess what they are saying?

Variation

- You can extend this activity to increase the number of cards the child selects. You may need a second bean bag or to throw it twice. Once the child has selected 2 cards, they have to use both parts of their body at once to communicate something.

** Activity 4: Talking body parts**

My hands

My face

My body

My arms

Activity 4: Talking body parts

My eyes

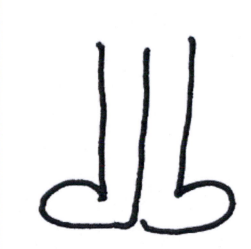

My legs

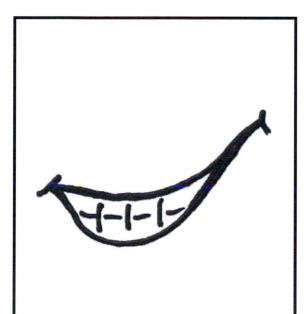

My mouth

My space

Activity 5: Our TALKABOUT rules

Preparation

Choose whether you want to use colour or black and white and print out the rules. You may also choose to enlarge the card.

You will want to laminate it so that it can be referred to every week.

Instructions

- Introduce the Talkabout rules. Explain that these are the areas that they are going to be thinking about for the next few sessions and that they can use this poster to help them every week.

- Good faces = good facial expression

- Good eyes = good eye contact

These will be covered together in '**Good Faces**'.

- Good bodies = good sitting, no fidgeting, good gesture.

- Good space = good distance and good touch.

Our Talkabout Rules

1.    **Good faces!**

2.    **Good eyes!**

3.    **Good body!**

4.    **Good space!**

39

Topic 2

 Topic 2: Talking faces

Objectives	To introduce facial expression and eye contact
	To understand the importance of using our faces and eyes when talking to people
	To help the children improve their use of facial expression and eye contact
Materials	You will need to print out and copy a number of the activities
	Some of the activities can be enlarged to A3
	Some of the activities are best laminated so that you can use them again
	You will also need blindfolds and thick card
Timing	This topic will take up to 9 sessions to complete.

Topic 2: Talking faces

Activity	Teacher notes
The blindfold game (Activity 6)	The children try to have a conversation using blindfolds. They then discuss what was difficult about it.
Find a face (Activity 7)	The children collect a number of faces showing different emotions from magazines or the internet and make a collage of facial expressions.
Bingo faces (Activity 8)	A bingo game using different facial expressions.
Making masks (Activity 9)	The children make masks to show different emotions and these are then used in the next activity.
Emotional sentences (Activity 10)	The facilitator says the prepared sentences using incorrect facial expression. The children identify what they should be looking like using the masks. They can then practise the sentence with and then without the masks.
Why are faces important? (Activity 11)	The group discuss why faces are important and they add their ideas to the brainstorm.
A story about faces (Activity 12)	Use the template to help the children complete a story about why faces are important.
Stop and stare (Activity 13)	An activity to practise good eye contact. The children walk around the room and when they are told to 'stop' they have to look at someone and ask them a question.
A day in the life (Activity 14)	The children create a story using the prepared sentences and they then act out the final story by using appropriate facial expressions.

41

Activity 6: The blindfold game

Preparation

Print out the topics for discussion.

Laminate the cards if you wish to use them again.

You will also need enough blindfolds for everyone in the group and a timer (optional).

Instructions

- Ask the children to choose a topic for discussion.

- Explain that we are going to spend 1 minute discussing the topic but they will all wear blindfolds so they will be unable to see one another in the group.

- When they have finished, ask them to take their blindfold off. What was difficult about the conversation?

- You can then divide the group into 2 teams. One team repeats the above task with another topic while the other team observes them. What did they notice about the conversation?

- You can then divide the group into pairs and ask one person to have a blindfold and the other one not. Repeat the exercise and ask them what was difficult.

- Ideas that the children will hopefully come up with are:

  - We need to be able to look at the other person
  - We need to use our faces to show how we are feeling
  - We need to show them that we are listening.
  - We need to watch the other person to see how they are feeling
  - We use our eyes and faces to help show that we want to speak (take turns)
  - It is polite to look at the person.

Find out what everyone had for dinner last night

Find out what everyone's favourite colour is

Find out what everyone did last weekend

Find out where everyone went for their last holiday

Find out what everyone's favourite television programme is

Find out what everyone's favourite meal is

Activity 7: Find a face

Preparation

Collect and print out a number of faces showing different emotions.

Print out the brainstorm page and enlarge to A3 or use a large piece of sugar paper.

You will also need scissors and glue.

Instructions

- Ask the children to pick a face from the pile and to place it on the brainstorm near the emotion that they think it is most like. If everyone agrees, the child then sticks the face to the large piece of paper.

- Continue the activity until you have faces that show at least 6 different emotions: happy, sad, angry, bored, scared and embarrassed.

Variation

- Create a collage on a piece of sugar paper using photos of different faces, placing them in different parts of the paper according to how they are feeling.

✿ Activity 7: Find a face

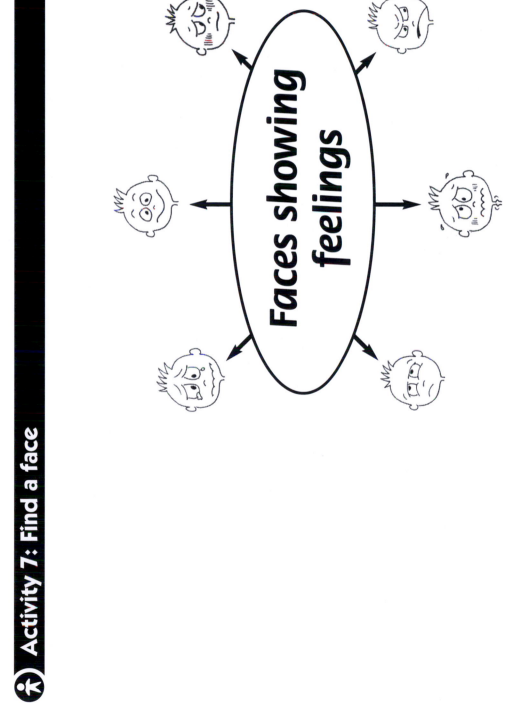

Faces showing feelings

ⓧ Activity 8: Bingo faces

Preparation

Print out and prepare the Bingo boards. (NB these are best in colour).

Prepare one board per child and laminate if you wish to use them again in the future.

Print out and prepare one set of the Bingo cards.

Prepare some plain cards, sticky notes or counters to use to cover up the Bingo pictures.

Instructions

- Every child has a Bingo board.

- The group facilitator has the pile of emotion cards and takes one at a time and makes the appropriate facial expression, e.g. a sad face.

- The children that think they have a sad face on their board then put their hands up. They then need to make a sad face and then they can cover it with a counter or piece of card.

- When all of their faces are covered, they call 'Bingo'.

Activity 8: Bingo faces

Happy

Sad

Excited

Bored

Worried

Embarrassed

Scared

Angry

Surprised

Hot

Tired

Cold

Activity 9: Making masks

Preparation

Print out and prepare the masks. These are best done in card if the children are going to hold them up to their faces. You may need to print out in paper and then stick the paper onto some card either before the children decorate them or afterwards. Make up a couple of each design.

You will need one mask for every emotion you want the children to draw.

You will also need a lolly stick or straw to attach to the masks to make it easier for the children to hold the masks up to their faces.

Instructions

- The group considers the facial expressions that they have been looking at and choose around 6 to draw. Try and get a good range of emotions, for example, happy, sad, angry, embarrassed, scared, worried etc.

- Each child chooses one emotion and a mask outline and decorates the mask to depict that emotion.

- The children may want to work in pairs to create their mask.

- Take photos of the children with the masks on and these can be made into a display.

Activity 9: Making masks

👤 Activity 10: Emotional sentences

Preparation

Print out the sentences.

You will also need the masks from the previous activity or the Bingo cards depicting emotions from activity 6.

Instructions

- The group facilitator chooses a sentence. They then say the sentence with the wrong facial expression, for example, 'my cat has just died' with a happy face.

- The children then have to identify the face that the facilitator was using and then identify the correct facial expression. This can be done by the children either pointing to the masks or to the Bingo cards.

- The facilitator then has to say the sentence again using the correct facial expression and all the children have a turn.

- They may like to use the masks to help them at first, and then to take the mask away and use their own face.

- They may like to make up their own sentences using their masks to show people how they are feeling.

- Are there any sentences that could be said in more than one way, depending on how the person was feeling? So there may be more than one right answer in some cases.

Activity 10: Emotional sentences

> My cat has just died

> I am going on holiday tomorrow

> Sometimes I hate my brother – he has just broken my favourite toy

> That film was the most frightening thing I have ever watched

> My friend has just given me a surprise present

> My mum wants me to go and talk to the new neighbours but I feel very shy

> I have to spend the whole of Sunday with my boring cousins – it's going to be awful

Activity 11: Why are faces important?

Preparation

Choose whether you want to use colour or black and white. Print out the worksheets and the cards.

Instructions

- Explain to the children that you are going to think about all the reasons why faces are important and what they have learned from the previous sessions.

- Use the pictures to help them and try to elicit the following:

  - To show people how we are feeling
  - To show people we are listening
  - To look at the other person to see how they are feeling
  - To use good eye contact
  - Using good eye contact is polite
  - To help take turns.

- They can then either cut out and stick the pictures onto the worksheet (which will need to be made A3) or they can write their ideas into the thought bubbles.

Activity 11: Why are faces important?

To show people how we are feeling

To show people that we are listening

To look at the other person to see how they are feeling

To use good eye contact when talking to people

Activity 11: Why are faces important?   Worksheet

Name _____   Date _____

Activity 12: A story about faces

Preparation

Choose whether you want to use colour or black and white. Print out the story template.

You will also need the photos of the children from activity 1, or pictures of different faces from the internet or cartoons from the previous activity.

You will also need scissors, glue and possibly colouring pens.

When the story is finished, you will need to laminate it or put it in plastic wallets to keep safe.

Instructions

- Tell the children you are going to write a story about faces. When they have written it, you are going to make it into a book to read.

Suggestions for the story

- Page 1 'My face is very important. It helps me to talk! This story is about good faces and good looking'
    - Illustrate using photos of the children or pictures of different faces

- Page 2 'My face is great! I use my face to...'
    - Suggestions: ... tell people how I am feeling; or show them I am interested; or show them I am listening
    - Illustrate with pictures of someone's face or cartoons

- Page 3 'People like it when I use good faces because...
    - Suggestions: ... they can see how I am feeling; or I will look interested in what they are saying
    - Illustrate with someone using a good expressive facial expression

- Page 4 'My eyes are great! I use my eyes to...'
    - Suggestions: ... show people I am listening; or to be polite
    - Illustrate with a photo of someone's eyes or a cartoon

Activity 12: A story about faces

Suggestions for the story continued

- Page 5 'People like it when I use good looking because...'
  - Suggestions: ... they will think I am polite; or they will know I am listening; or they will know I am interested
  - Illustrate with a photo of someone using good eye contact

- Page 6 'I will try to use good faces and good looking when I talk to people'
  - Illustrate with photos of the children using good faces and good looking

- Page 7 'My .... will be happy. My .... will be happy'
  - Suggestions: ... mum, teacher, friends, family
  - Illustrate with lots of people looking happy.

See CD for all relevant activity pages

Activity 13: Stop and stare

Preparation

Create some space in the room so that the children can move around freely.

Instructions

- Ask the children to move around the room. While the children are walking around the room, the facilitator will tell them the question they are to ask when they stop. Questions could be:
  - What is your favourite colour?
  - What did you have for breakfast?
  - What is your favourite animal?

- The group facilitator then calls 'STOP' and the children turn to the person nearest to them and ask them the question. They need to concentrate on making good eye contact and using good facial expression.

- The group facilitator looks out for good practice and encourages some children to show the rest of the group what they did.

- Repeat the activity until everyone is doing well and has been praised.

Activity 14: A day in the life

Preparation

Choose the story you want to use and cut out the sentences.

Print out the story board. You may want to enlarge this to A3 so that the children can see it better. You may also want to laminate it and stick the sentences to it using Velcro.

You may want to laminate them if you are going to use this activity again.

Instructions

- Explain to the children that they are going to create a story using sentences.

- Each sentence has an emotion attached to it and so will need an appropriate facial expression.

- Place the sentences in the middle of the group face down or in a feely bag.

- The children take it in turns to pick up a sentence and place it on the card.

- When all the sentences are there, the facilitator reads the story and the children join in by adding in the appropriate facial expressions at the end of each sentence. You may also encourage them to use gesture and noises to make the story funnier.

- You may choose to tell the story again with someone else being the narrator or to re-order the sentences.

Activity 14: A day in the life   Story 1 Christmas Day

I had the happiest Christmas day!

(very happy 'hooray!')

I woke up very early and found that Father Christmas had been in the night and left me lots of presents

(excited 'yippee!')

The best present I got was a new cool bike from my mum and dad

(very happy 'cool!')

Unfortunately it was pouring with rain so I couldn't go outside

(disappointed / sad 'ooh!')

Some boring relatives came for a drink and they talked and talked and talked

(bored 'boring!')

The funniest thing was when the dog knocked the Christmas tree over

(funny 'oh no!')

My dad got very cross with the dog who also tried to eat the turkey

(angry 'no!')

But I was so tired at the end of the day, I fell asleep in front of the television

(tired 'snore!')

59

Activity 14: A day in the life

✂️

Sentence 1

Sentence 2

Sentence 3

Sentence 4

Sentence 5

Sentence 6

Sentence 7

Sentence 8

Topic 3: Talking bodies

Objectives

To introduce posture

To understand the importance of posture and gesture when talking to people

To help the children improve their use of posture and gesture and discourage the use of fidgeting

Materials

You will need to print out and copy a number of the activities

Some of the activities can be enlarged to A3

Some of the activities are best laminated so that you can use them again

Timing

This topic will take up to 6 sessions to complete.

Topic 3: Talking bodies

Activity	Teacher notes
Walk this way! (Activity 15)	The children walk around the room using their bodies in different ways to express different feelings.
Posture thermometer (Activity 16)	The children consider posture according to a tense thermometer and think about what you notice when people are tense and relaxed.
When we are tense/ relaxed… (Activity 17)	The children consider what happens when they are tense / relaxed and how they might be feeling.
Why are bodies important? (Activity 18)	The group discuss why bodies are important and they add their ideas to the brainstorm.
A story about our bodies (Activity 19)	Use the template to help the children complete a story about why bodies are important when talking to other people.
Give us a hand (Activity 20)	An activity to practise good use of body language and gesture. The children have to act out scenarios using gesture and body movements and the others have to guess what is on their card.

Activity 15: Walk this way!

Preparation

Clear enough space in the room to allow the children to move around freely.

You will also need a camera to take photos of the children (if possible).

Instructions

- Explain to the children that they are going to stand up and think about their bodies. The facilitator then gives them the following instructions:

- Make yourselves as **tall** as possible – raise your head, straighten your back etc. Stop and look around the room – how do we all look?

- Make yourselves as **small** as possible – huddle into a ball, bring your head down etc. Stop and look around the room – how do we all look?

- Imagine that you are really **angry** – make your body and face look angry and then walk across the room. Stop and look around the room – how do we all look? Take a photo of a couple of the children.

- Imagine that you are really **excited** – what might you do if you're excited? Move around the room a bit and show the others you are very excited. Stop and look around the room – how do we all look? Take a photo of a couple of the children.

- Imagine that you are really **sleepy** – make your body and face look sleepy and then walk across the room. Find a chair and sit down. Stop and look around the room – how do we all look? Take a photo of a couple of the children.

- Imagine that you are really **embarrassed** – make your body and face look embarrassed. Move around the room and show others that you are embarrassed about something. Stop and look around the room – how do we all look? Take a photo of a couple of the children.

- Other emotions that are good to do are: **scared**, **happy** and **nervous**. Ask the children to think about how they changed their posture according to how they were feeling. Introduce the terms **tense** and **relaxed**.

Activity 16: Posture thermometer

Preparation

Print out the thermometer – this is best enlarged to A3.

You will also need pictures of different emotions. You can use the photos of the children taken in the last activity, or photos of other people looking angry, excited, sleepy etc, or the emotion bingo cards from activity 8.

Instructions

- Show the children the thermometer and explain that sometimes our bodies are really tense and sometimes they are really relaxed and sometimes we are in the middle.

- Ask them to sit in a really tense posture (number 5), then in a really relaxed posture (number 1) and then in a normal posture (number 3).

- Look at the pictures of the different emotions – where do you think they would go on the thermometer?

- The children then stick the emotions onto the thermometer according to what they see, for example an angry posture will be either at 4 or 5 and a sleepy posture will be a 1 or a 2.

- This activity can be done as a large group around the one thermometer or in pairs using worksheets.

🧍 Activity 16: Posture thermometer

5

4

3

2

1

Activity 17: When we are tense / relaxed...

Preparation

Print out the worksheets – these can be enlarged to A3 if necessary.

You will also need scissors and glue.

Instructions

- Ask the children to think about being tense (4 or a 5) – what happens to their body?

- The children then cut and stick the pictures that they think may go with being tense and add them to the worksheet.

- They then think about what other people may think if they see someone who is very tense.

- They then think about nice and relaxed (2 or a 3) – what happens to their body when they are nice and relaxed?

- The children then cut and stick the pictures that they think may go with being relaxed and add them to the worksheet.

- They then think about what other people may think if they see someone who is nice and relaxed.

Activity 17: When we are tense...

Upright posture

Relaxed posture

Tense sitting

Good sitting

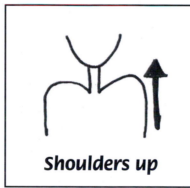

Shoulders up

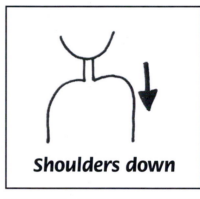

Shoulders down

Clenched fist

Fidgeting

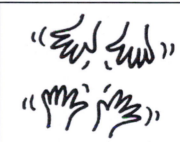

Too much gesture

Good use of gesture

Sweaty hands

Relaxed hands

67

★ Activity 18: Why are bodies important?

Preparation

Choose whether you want to use colour or black and white. Print out the worksheets and the cards.

Instructions

- Explain to the children that you are going to think about all the reasons why good posture and gesture are important when talking to someone and what they have learnt from the previous activities.

- Use the pictures to help them and try to elicit the following:

  - To show people how we are feeling
  - To show people we are listening and interested
  - To help us pay attention and listen
  - To be polite
  - To show people we care for them
  - To help us explain something.

- They can then either cut out and stick the pictures onto the worksheet (which will need to be made A3) or they can write their ideas into the thought bubbles.

Activity 18: Why are bodies important?

To show people how we are feeling

To show people that we are listening and interested

To help us pay attention and listen

To be polite

Sometimes to show people that we care for them

To help us explain something

Activity 18: Why are bodies important? Worksheet

Name _____ Date _____

Activity 19: A story about our bodies

Preparation

Choose whether you want to use colour or black and white. Print out the story template.

You will need the photos of the children from activity 15, or pictures of different postures etc from the internet or cartoons from previous activities.

You will also need scissors, glue and possibly colouring pens.

When the story is finished, you will need to laminate it or put it in plastic wallets to keep it safe.

Instructions

- Tell the children you are going to write a story about our bodies. When they have written it, you are going to make it into a book to read.

Suggestions for the story

- Page 1 'My body is very important. It helps me to talk! This is called body language. This story is about good sitting and good hands.'
  - Illustrate using photos of the children or pictures of different people

- Page 2 'My body is great! I use my body to do good sitting. This ...'
  - Suggestions: ... shows people how I am feeling; or shows them I am interested; or shows them I am listening
  - Illustrate with pictures of someone's body posture/gesture or cartoons

- Page 3 'People like it when I use good sitting because...
  - Suggestions: ... they can see I am listening; or it's polite; it helps me pay attention to what they are saying
  - Illustrate with someone using good sitting

- Page 4 'My hands are great! I use my hands to...'
  - Suggestions: ... help me explain things; or to show someone I care; or to be polite
  - Illustrate with a photo of someone's hands or a cartoon

 Activity 19: A story about our bodies

Suggestions for the story continued

- Page 5 'People like it when I use good hands because...'
    - Suggestions: ... they will think I am polite; or it helps them understand me
    - Illustrate with a photo of someone using good gesture

- Page 6 'I will try to use good sitting and good hands when I talk to people'
    - Illustrate with photos of the children using good sitting and good gestures

- Page 7 'My .... will be happy. My .... will be happy'
    - Suggestions: ... mum, teacher, friends, family
    - Illustrate with lots of people looking happy.

 Activity 20: Give us a hand

Preparation

Print out the cards and laminate if you want to use them again.

Instructions

- Explain to the children that you are going to practise some of their good body language by acting out scenarios to the group.

- They may like to do this in pairs.

- Firstly they mime the action and the group tries to guess what is on their card.

- When they have correctly guessed the statement, the child(ren) do the acting again but this time with words. The other children may like to give suggestions for what they could say.

- What is good about acting when we use words and good body language?

See CD for all relevant activity pages

Activity 20: Give us a hand

I have eaten too much and now I feel really ill

Can you be quiet? It is very noisy in here and I have a headache

I have just watched a very scary film and now I am frightened and don't want to go to bed

I am watching football on TV and my favourite team have just scored a goal!

I am going for a walk and suddenly it starts to rain and I have to run for cover

I have lost my cat – I have tried calling him but I can't find him.
Have you seen him?

Topic 4

Topic 4: Talking space

Objectives   To introduce distance and touch

To understand the importance of space when talking to people

To help the children improve their use of distance and space

Materials   You will need to print out and copy a number of the activities

Some of the activities can be enlarged to A3

Some of the activities are best laminated so that you can use them again

Timing   This topic will take up to 5 sessions to complete.

👤 Topic 4: Talking space

Activity	Teacher notes
Space control (Activity 21)	An activity to find out how close we can get to different people.
Touch control (Activity 22)	The children consider different kinds of touch and whether we can use that kind of touch with certain people.
What happens when... (Activity 23)	The children consider what happens when they get it wrong – how will people feel or react?
A story about space (Activity 24)	Use the template to help the children complete a story about why space is important when talking to other people.
Space hoppers (Activity 25)	An activity to practise good use of space. The children move around the room to show what kinds of touch they would use in different situations.
Certificate of achievement (Activity 26)	The children receive a certificate to celebrate their achievement. This could be their laminated record of achievement if this has been used throughout the sessions or the other general certificate for completing the level.

Activity 21: Space control

Preparation

You will need a very large piece of paper (I use 4 pieces of flip chart paper stuck together) with 2 circles drawn on it in a similar manner to the worksheet. Draw a pair of feet in the middle of one of the short edges.

Print out worksheets.

You may also want to use a camera.

Instructions

- Explain to the children that you are going to think about how close we can get to people.

- Ask one child to stand on the drawn feet.

- Ask someone else to go up and stand where they both feel comfortable. When they have agreed, draw another pair of feet where the second child stood and write their names, e.g. 'Jenny and Amy'. You may like to take a photo.

- You can also ask them to hold out their arms and see whether they are 1 arms length away (a standard rule for distance). You may like to take a photo of this to use later in activity 24.

- Then ask another child to come up and repeat the exercise.

- Continue until everyone has had a turn at standing on the feet and standing in the circles.

- Are there any differences? Was anyone closer than 1 arms length? Why was that? (Close friends?)

- Who can stand in your inner circle?

- The children then complete their worksheet and try to think of a few people to put in each of their circles.

77

Level 1 TALKABOUT Body Language

Activity 21: Space control — Worksheet

Name _____ Date _____

Who can I get close to? Can I think of a few people in each circle?

not so close to...

quite close to...

very close to...

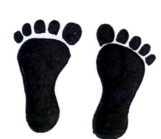

Activity 22: Touch control

Preparation

You will need to make up the 2 sets of cards. These can be cut out and laminated if you want to use them again.

You may like to play this with 2 dice. You will need 2 square tissue boxes and you can then attach each picture to one side of the tissue box. You will need to make 2 dice – one with the types of touch and one with the people on it.

Photocopy the worksheet.

You will also need scissors and glue.

Instructions

- Explain to the children that you are going to think about different types of touch and whether we can use that touch with certain people.

- Create 2 piles of cards – one for touch and one for the people.

- Alternatively have 2 dice.

- Ask one child to select one picture from one pile and another picture from the second pile or to throw the 2 dice.

- The child then considers whether they can 'kiss' 'their teacher' or 'high five' 'an adult I don't know well'.

- Continue playing until everyone has had a turn and all combinations have been explored.

- The children could then complete the worksheet. This could be done in pairs. The children consider the different types of touch and cut and stick what they could do with the different people.

Activity 22: Touch control

High Five

Pat on back

Shake hands

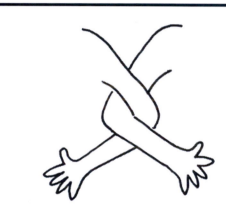

Link arms

Hug

Kiss

Activity 22: Touch control

My mum or dad

My best friend

My teachers

A class mate

My brother or sister

An adult I don't know well

 Activity 23: What happens when...

Preparation

Print out and photocopy the worksheets. You may like to reuse the Bingo emotion cards again (activity 8).

You will also need scissors and glue.

Instructions

- Ask the children to think about what would happen if we got it wrong. See if the children can come up with some examples, for example hugging a teacher. How do they think the other person will feel?

- Go through the different emotions (you can use the Bingo emotion cards from activity 8 if you want) and see how many could be true. They might find it easier to think about if someone they didn't know well gave them a hug, how would they feel? Go through the emotions and test each one out. Would you feel 'happy'? Would you feel 'embarrassed'? Would you feel 'cold'? etc.

- Ask the children to think about what would happen when we get it right. How do they think the other person will feel?

- The children then complete the worksheet and cut and stick the emotions that they think are possible.

- They may want to add some of their own that are not illustrated.

82

Activity 23: What happens when...

Happy

Sad

Excited

Bored

Worried

Embarrassed

Scared

Angry

Surprised

Hot

Tired

Cold

Activity 24: A story about space

Preparation

Choose whether you want to use colour or black and white. Print out the story template.

You can also use the photos of the children from activity 21, and pictures of people using different forms of touch from the internet.

You will also need scissors, glue and possibly colouring pens.

When the story is finished, you will need to laminate it or put it in plastic wallets to keep safe.

Instructions

- Tell the children you are going to write a story about space. When they have written it, you are going to make it into a book to read.

- Only use the pages on the different types of touch that are appropriate to your group (pages 5-9).

Suggestions for the story

- Page 1 'Space is very important. It helps me to talk! This story is about good space and good touch.'
    - Illustrate using photos of the children or pictures of different people

- Page 2 'Touching and hugging is special. It means we get very close to someone. Lots of people touch and hug...'
    - Suggestions: ... married people, girlfriend and boyfriend, mum and child, close friends
    - Illustrate with pictures of people hugging

- Page 3 'Getting too close to other people will make them feel...'
    - Suggestions: ... embarrassed, angry, nervous
    - Illustrate with cartoons of emotions

Activity 24: A story about space

Suggestions for the story continued

- Page 4 'People like it when I use good space because…'
  - Suggestions: … they feel happy; I'm being polite
  - Illustrate with a photo of the children demonstrating good distance

- Page 5 'I can hug…' (optional page)
  - Suggestions: … my mum, dad, best friend
  - Illustrate with a photo or cartoon of someone hugging

- Page 6 'I can link arms with…' (optional page)
  - Suggestions: … best friend
  - Illustrate with a photo or cartoon of someone linking arms

- Page 7 'I can hold hands with…' (optional page)
  - Suggestions: … my mum, dad, boyfriend, girlfriend
  - Illustrate with a photo or cartoon of someone holding hands

- Page 8 'I can high five…' (optional page)
  - Suggestions: … my friends at school, cousins
  - Illustrate with a photo or cartoon of someone doing a high five

- Page 9 'I can shake hands with…' (optional page)
  - Suggestions: … adults I don't know well, the head teacher
  - Illustrate with a photo or cartoon of someone shaking hands

- Page 10 'I will try to use good space when I talk to people'
  - Illustrate with photos of the children using good distance

- Page 11 'My ………. will be happy. My …………. will be happy'
  - Suggestions: … mum, teacher, friends, family
  - Illustrate with lots of people looking happy.

See CD for all relevant activity pages

85

 Activity 25: Space hoppers

Preparation

Choose whether you want to use colour or black and white. Print out the 'touch' cards from Activity 22 and the 2 extra ones. You may want to enlarge them to A4 or A3. Print out the situation cards.

You will also need to create some space for the children to move around the room.

Instructions

- Remind the children of the 6 ways they have talked about in terms of touching people:
  - High five
  - Hug
  - Kiss
  - Link arms
  - Shake hands
  - Pat on back.

- Talk about the 2 other cards: sometimes we choose not to touch and to just stand near to the person and sometimes we do something else, e.g. hold hands.

- Place the 8 cards around the room.

- Read out a scenario and ask the children to move to the part of the room that is right for them. If they would do something different then they are to go to the card that says 'something else?'

- Explain that there may be several different right answers so they should try and make the decision for them and not be influenced by where everyone else is going.

- Discuss the differences and the similarities.

- Can the children think of any other scenarios?

Activity 25: Space hoppers

Stand near to

Something else?

You are crossing a busy road with your mum

You are being introduced to a new teacher

Your grandad arrives for the weekend

A new child starts at your school and you go and say hello

 Activity 25: Space hoppers

You see your best friend in town	Your best friend has just given you a great birthday present
Your friend is upset	Your teacher looks upset
Your dad has just got home from work and you go to say hello	Your granny is not well and you go to visit her in hospital
Your sister arrives home after being away for 3 months	The Headteacher wants to see you so you go to her office

Activity 26: Certificate of achievement

Preparation

Print out the certificates and laminate if possible.

Instructions

- Give the children their certificate with a round of applause!

Contents   C/V*   Page

Topic 1: Talkabout talking

Topic 2: Talkabout speaking

Topic 3: Talkabout listening

Topic 4: Talkabout beginnings

Topic 5: Talkabout taking turns

Topic 6: Talkabout endings

*C/V = colour version of worksheet available on the CD

Introduction

Aim of this level	To increase awareness of conversational skills and to improve skills in using speaking and listening in conversations effectively.
Topics covered	1. Talkabout talking 2. Talkabout speaking 3. Talkabout listening 4. Talkabout beginnings 5. Talkabout turn taking 6. Talkabout endings.
Materials	A number of the activities throughout this level use a couple of characters called Gary and Brad. I suggest that you purchase or borrow a couple of puppets or soft toys.
Length of level	This level will take up to 24 lessons depending on the ability of the students and the length of the lessons.
Students	Groups work best if the children get on and are well matched for both personality and need. Aim for a group of between 4 and 8 people. Remember that a larger group will mean the level may take longer to complete.
Group gelling	Factors that can help group cohesion are: group cohesion activities (see pages 247–48); getting the group to decide on a name for the group; devising some group rules; making sure everyone takes part; and good leadership.
Format of the sessions	1. Group cohesion activity 2. Recap 3. Main activity(s) 4. Group cohesion activity .
Confidentiality	Remind everyone that the content of the sessions is not to be discussed with other students outside of the session.

92

👤 Topic 1: Talkabout talking

Objectives: To introduce conversational skills and the way we talk

To gel the group

To introduce the importance of the way we talk and the 4 key areas of conversations: listening, starting a conversation, taking turns and ending a conversation. The skills of relevance, asking and answering a question and repair are covered within the existing topics

Materials: You will need a couple of puppets or soft toys for the characters 'Brad' and 'Gary'

You will need to print out and copy a number of the activities

Some of the activities are best enlarged to A3

Some of the activities are best laminated so that you can use them again

You may need a bean bag for one activity

Timing: This topic will take up to 3 sessions to complete.

Topic 1: Talkabout talking

Activity	Teacher notes
A puppet show (Activity 1)	A series of 'puppet shows' to introduce the topics that are important within conversations: speaking, listening, beginnings, turn taking and endings.
Our TALKABOUT rules (Activity 2)	A poster is prepared for the children to refer to for the rest of the level.

Activity 1: A puppet show

Preparation

You will need 2 puppets or soft toys (teddies or animals can work fine). One will be 'Gary' and one will be 'Brad'.

Print out the scripts and the Talkabout Rules.

Print and cut out enough 'good' and 'bad' cards for everyone to have a set.

Print and cut out 1 card of each of the 5 rules.

Laminate the scripts, cards and the rules if you wish to use them again.

Instructions

- You will need 2 facilitators: one to hold Gary and one to hold Brad.

- Introduce the children to Brad and Gary. I usually do this through the puppets saying a few words such as:

Brad	Hello my name is Brad
Gary	Hello my name is Gary
Brad	Hello Gary
Gary	Hello Brad
B & G	We're best friends
Brad	We like talking to each other
Gary	But sometimes we get it wrong
Brad	Would you like to help us get it right?

- Give everyone a 'good' card and a 'bad' card and explain that at the end of every conversation they are going to decide whether they were good or bad.

- Use Brad and Gary to act out each scenario and then ask the children to rate whether it was good or bad.

- Ask them to tell you what was wrong, e.g. 'not a good voice'; 'speaking too loud' etc. Introduce the symbol for 'good speaking'.

- Brad and Gary then act out the scenario using good speaking etc.

- Continue through the 5 scenarios until the children have identified the 5 key learning points: good speaking; good listening; good beginnings; good turn taking; good endings.

Activity 1: A puppet show

Act 1 'Bad speaking'

Brad	(shouting) HELLO GARY!
Gary	(jumps) Brad! You scared me!
Brad	(very quietly) Sorry!
Gary	What?
Brad	I said sorry
Gary	What do you want Brad?
Brad	(very fast rate) Do you want to go to the park to play football?
Gary	I can't understand what you are saying!
Brad	(very slow rate) Do… you… want… to… go… to… the… park… to… play… football?
Gary	Ok Brad, let's go
Brad	(shouting) GREAT!
Gary	(jumps) Brad!

Act 1 'Good speaking'

(use picture for 'good speaking')

Brad	Hello Gary
Gary	Hello Brad
Brad	Do you want to go to the park to play football?
Gary	Yes! Good idea – let's go!
Brad	Great!

Activity 1: A puppet show

Act 2 'Bad listening'

Brad	Hello Gary
Gary	Hello Brad
Brad	How are you today Gary?
Gary	I'm not very happy today. My mum is very cross with me and I'm not allowed to go out to play (sniff) and…
Brad	(Obviously not listening) Yeah, yeah… anyway, do you want to go to the park to play football?
Gary	Uh? But I just told you I'm not allowed!
Brad	Ok – I'll meet you at the park in 5 minutes. Bye!
Gary	Brad!

Act 2 'Good listening'

(use picture for 'good listening')

Brad	Hello Gary
Gary	Hello Brad
Brad	How are you today Gary?
Gary	I'm not very happy today. My mum is very cross with me and I'm not allowed to go out to play
Brad	Oh no, I'm sorry. I was going to ask you to come and play football
Gary	Oh… maybe tomorrow?
Brad	That's a good idea. Let's play tomorrow.
Gary	OK. Bye!
Brad	Bye!

🧍 Activity 1: A puppet show

Act 3 'Bad beginnings part 1'

Narrator Brad wants to talk to Gary.

Gary   (Gary is facing the other way – his back is towards Brad)

Brad   (Approaches Gary and just stands there) um…

Gary   (Turns around) What?

Brad   um…

Gary   Brad?

Brad   um… (Walks off)

Gary   Uh?

Act 3 'Bad beginnings part 2'

Gary   (Gary is facing the other way – his back is towards Brad)

Brad   (Approaches Gary's back) Do you want to go to the park to play football?

Gary   (Jumps and turns around) What? Oh hello Brad.

Brad   Yeah – do you want to go to the park to play football?

Gary   Oh… OK.

Act 3 'Good beginnings'

(use picture for 'good beginnings')

Gary   (Gary is facing the other way – his back is towards Brad)

Brad   (Approaches Gary's back) Hello Gary!

Gary   (Turns around) Oh hello Brad.

Brad   Do you want to go to the park to play football?

Gary   Yes! Good idea – let's go!

Brad   Great!

Activity 1: A puppet show

Act 4 'Bad turn taking''

Brad   Hello Gary

Gary   Hello Brad

Brad   How are you today Gary?

(Talking at same time)

Gary }   I'm not very happy today. My mum is very cross with me

Brad }   I was wondering if you want to go to the park to play football?

(Talking at same time)

Gary }   Uh?

Brad }   Uh?

(Talking at same time)

Gary }   My mum says I am not allowed to go out to play

Brad }   It's a nice day to go to the park, isn't it?

(Talking at same time)

Gary }   Uh?

Brad }   Uh?

Act 4 'Good turn taking'

(use picture for 'good turn taking')

Brad   Hello Gary

Gary   Hello Brad

Brad   How are you today Gary?

Gary   I'm not very happy today. My mum is very cross with me and
          I'm not allowed to go out to play

Brad   Oh no, I'm sorry. I was going to ask you to come and play
          football

Gary   Oh… maybe tomorrow?

Brad   That's a good idea. Let's play tomorrow.

Gary   OK. Bye!

Brad   Bye!

👤 Activity 1: A puppet show

Act 5 'Bad endings'

Brad	Hello Gary
Gary	Hello Brad
Brad	How are you today Gary?
Gary	I'm not very happy today. My mum is very cross with me and I'm not allowed to go out to play
Brad	Oh no, I'm sorry. What happened?
Gary	Well, my mum is cross with me because I haven't tidied my room and…
Brad	(Walking off) Got to go, see you later!
Gary	Brad!

Act 5 'Good endings'

(use picture for 'good endings')

Brad	Hello Gary
Gary	Hello Brad
Brad	How are you today Gary?
Gary	I'm not very happy today. My mum is very cross with me and I'm not allowed to go out to play.
Brad	What happened?
Gary	Well, my mum is cross with me because I haven't tidied my room.
Brad	Oh no, I'm sorry. I was going to ask you to come and play football
Gary	Oh… maybe tomorrow?
Brad	That's a good idea. Let's play tomorrow.
Gary	OK. Bye!
Brad	Bye!

Activity 1: A puppet show

Good

Bad

Good

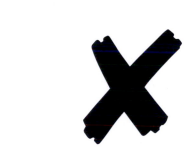

Bad

Good

Bad

Activity 1: A puppet show

Good speaking

Good listening

Good beginnings

Good turn taking

Good endings

Activity 2: Our TALKABOUT rules

Preparation

Choose whether you want to use colour or black and white and print out the rules. You may also choose to enlarge the card.

You will want to laminate it so that it can be referred to every week.

Instructions

- Introduce the Talkabout rules. Explain that these are the areas that they are going to be thinking about for the next few sessions and that they can use this poster to help them every week.

- **Good speaking** = good volume, rate and intonation

- **Good listening** = good body language and good commenting

- **Good beginnings** = starting the conversation appropriately

- **Good turn taking** = taking turns in a conversation by asking and answering questions and talking about relevant things

- **Good endings** = ending the conversation appropriately.

Our TALKABOUT talking rules

1. Talk, talk, talk, talk, talk, talk **Good speaking!**

2. **Good listening!**

3. Hello **Good beginnings!**

4. **Good turn taking!**

5. Bye **Good endings!**

Topic 2: Talkabout speaking

Objectives: To introduce volume and rate and 'good speaking'

To understand the importance of a good voice when talking to people

To help the children improve their use of volume and rate and where appropriate, intonation, fluency and clarity

Materials: You will need the Gary and Brad puppets

You will need to print out and copy a number of the activities

Some of the activities can be enlarged to A3

Some of the activities are best laminated so that you can use them again

You may also need bean bags

Timing: This topic will take up to 5 sessions to complete.

👤 Topic 2: Talkabout speaking

Activity	Teacher notes
Talking to Gary (Activity 3)	The children take it in turns to hold either Gary or Brad. The person holding Brad then asks Gary a question using different voices. These are chosen either by using bean bags on a mat or selecting a card.
Turn up the volume (Activity 4)	The children consider volume and when it is appropriate to use a quiet or loud voice.
Racing rates (Activity 5)	The children consider rate of speech and how it can vary according to how we are feeling.
Why is good speaking important? (Activity 6)	The group discuss why good speaking is important and they add their ideas to the brainstorm.
Gary and Brad have a chat (Activity 7)	An activity to practise good speaking. The children use Gary and Brad to have a conversation and to practise their skills.

Activity 3: Talking to Gary

Preparation

You will need the Gary and Brad puppets and the 'good speaking' card from the previous topic.

Decide whether you want to use colour or black and white cards. Print out and cut up. Laminate if you want to use them again.

To simplify the activity use 2 bean bags and make up 2 mats using the cards you have printed out. Each mat should be made up with 4 coloured A5 pieces of paper stuck together to make an A3 mat. Laminate to make it reusable. Stick the cards to the mat using Blu Tack or Velcro strips.

Instructions

- Ask the children to take it in turns to hold Gary and Brad.

- Explain that the child holding Brad will ask the child holding Gary a question and will use a different kind of voice. They will then repeat the question using a good voice.

- The child holding Brad throws the bean bag onto the mat to select how they are going to speak. Alternatively they select a card.

- The child holding Gary throws their bean bag onto the other mat to select the question. Alternatively they select one of the four cards.

- Brad then asks Gary the question using that voice.

- The group talk about how it sounded and then Brad asks the question again using a good voice.

- The children then pass the 2 puppets to other children in the group and the activity continues.

** Activity 3: Talking to Gary**

Slow

Fast

Quiet

Loud

Activity 3: Talking to Gary

What's your favourite food?

What's your favourite animal?

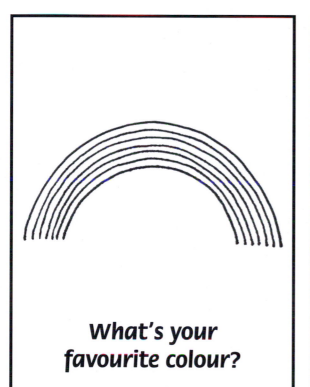

What's your favourite colour?

What's your favourite weather?

Activity 4: Turn up the volume

Preparation

You will need to print out and make up the rating scale and cards. The rating scale is best laminated with a Velcro strip along the bottom so that cards can be placed along the scale. Velcro will then need to be attached to the back of the cards.

Instructions

- Introduce the rating scale to the children.

- Explain that sometimes we have to use loud voices and sometimes we have to use quiet voices.

- Ask the children to take it in turns to pick up a card and to think about the scenario. Do they need to use a quiet voice, normal voice or loud voice in that situation? They then place the card along the rating scale.

- What might they say in that situation? And how would they say it?

- The activity continues until all the cards have been used.

- Can the children think of any other situations when they may use a loud or quiet voice?

My Volume...

Very quiet

Good volume

Very loud

1 . . . . 2 . . . . 3 . . . . 4 5

👤 Activity 4: Turn up the volume

In the library

In a cinema

At a rock concert

At a party

In class

In the playground

In church

At the football

Talking to a friend

Talking to a teacher

When someone is sleeping

In a shop

Activity 5: Racing rates

Preparation

You will need to print out and make up the rating scale and cards. The rating scale is best laminated with a Velcro strip along the bottom so that cards can be placed along the scale. Velcro will then need to be attached to the back of the cards.

Instructions

- Introduce the rating scale to the children.

- Explain that sometimes we speak fast and sometimes we speak slowly.

- Ask the children to take it in turns to pick up a card and to think about the emotion on the card. Do they think they speak slowly or fast when they are feeling like that? They then place the card along the rating scale.

- What might they say when they are feeling that emotion? Can they give an example and show people how they would say it.

- The activity continues until all the cards have been used.

- Can the children think of any other situations when they may use fast or slow speech?

My Rate...

Very slow

Good rate

Very fast

1 ········· 2 ········· 3 ········· 4 ········· 5

Activity 5: Racing rates

Sad

Excited

Happy

Angry

Bored

Nervous

Sleepy

Surprised

👤 Activity 6: Why is good speaking important?

Preparation

Choose whether you want to use colour or black and white. Print out the worksheets and the cards.

Instructions

- Explain to the children that you are going to think about all the reasons why good speaking is important and what they have learnt from the previous sessions.

- Use the pictures to help them and try to elicit the following:

  - To help people understand what we are saying
  - To show people how we are feeling
  - To show people we are interested
  - To be polite
  - To help people want to talk to us
  - To make conversations easier.

- They can then either cut out and stick the pictures onto the worksheet (which will need to be made A3) or they can write their ideas into the thought bubbles.

Activity 6: Why is good speaking important?

To show people how we are feeling

To help people understand what we are saying

To show people we are interested

To be polite

To help people want to talk to us

To make conversations easier

Activity 7: Gary and Brad have a chat

Preparation

You will need the Gary and Brad puppets or an alternative.

You will need to print out the 6 scenarios for the children. Cut out and laminate if you want to use them again.

Instructions

- Explain to the children that they are going to practise their good speaking using the Gary and Brad puppets.

- The children take it in turns to be Gary and Brad and they prepare a short conversation about one of the topics:
  - Gary and Brad are planning a sleep over at the weekend
  - Gary and Brad are talking about going back to school after the holidays
  - Gary and Brad are talking about what to do after school
  - Gary and Brad are talking about what they are going to eat for supper
  - Gary and Brad are talking about their summer holidays and where they are going to go
  - The children choose the topic.

- You may choose to use the picture for 'good speaking' or the rating scales for rate and volume if you think the children may benefit from them.

- Discuss how they did. Do they think they did good speaking? Could they have improved any part? If so, ask them to replay that part.

- Gary and Brad take a bow and the group give them a round of applause!

Activity 7: Gary and Brad have a chat

You are planning a sleep over at the weekend. What are you going to do?

You are talking about going back to school after the holidays

You are planning what you could do together after school

You are talking about what you are going to have for supper this evening

You are talking about your summer holidays and what you are going to do

You choose! What would you like to talk about?

Topic 3

Topic 3: Talkabout listening

Objectives:　　To introduce the skills involved in 'good listening'

To understand the importance of listening when talking to people

To help the children improve their listening skills

Materials:　　You will need to print out and copy a number of the activities

Some of the activities can be enlarged to A3

Some of the activities are best laminated so that you can use them again

Timing:　　This topic will take up to 3 sessions to complete.

Topic 3: Talkabout listening

Activity	Teacher notes
Back to back (Activity 8)	The children have a conversation back to back and see why it is more difficult to listen. Introduce the 4 main aspects to listening: good looking, good faces, good bodies and good comments.
Good commenting (Activity 9)	The group practise what a good comment means. They practise this by listening to different sentences and using the different comments. The group then try to match the sentence with the right comment.
Face to face (Activity 10)	An activity to practise good listening. The children use the same topics in 'back to back' (activity 8) and the four rules to good listening to practise their listening skills. The group use the 'good listening' rating scale to consider how they did.

 Activity 8: Back to back

Preparation

Print out the topics for discussion.

Laminate the cards if you wish to use them again.

You will also need to place 2 chairs back to back.

Instructions

- This is a similar activity to the blindfold game in level 1. Ask the children to get into pairs and to choose a topic to talk about.

- Explain that they are going to spend 1 minute discussing the topic but they will be back to back.

- You may choose to do this one pair at a time with the other children observing or to do it simultaneously.

- When they have finished, ask them why it was difficult to listen? What does good listening mean?

- Ideas that the children will hopefully come up with are:
  - We need to be able to look at the other person
  - We need to use our faces to show them that we are listening
  - We need to use our bodies (posture) to show them we are interested and listening
  - We need to make comments and ask relevant questions to show them we are listening.

- Introduce the 4 aspects of good listening
  - Good looking
  - Good faces
  - Good bodies
  - Good comments.

Activity 8: Back to back

> ### Find out what your partner had for dinner last night

> ### Find out what your partner's favourite colour is and why

> ### Find out what your partner did last weekend

> ### Find out where your partner went for their last holiday

> ### Find out what your partner's favourite television programme is

> ### Find out what your partner's favourite meal is

Our GOOD LISTENING rules

1.  **Good looking!**

2. **Good faces!**

3. **Good bodies!**

4. **Good comments!**

Really?
Oh No!

 Activity 9: Good commenting

Preparation

Print out the sentences and comment cards.

Laminate the cards if you wish to use them again.

Instructions

- Place the comment cards in the centre of the circle face down.

- Explain that they are going to take it in turns to listen to a sentence and then to comment on what has been said using one of the comment cards.

- The group leader then says one of the sentences and one person selects a comment card and reads the comment. What did everyone think about the comment? Was it appropriate?

- When all the sentences have been read and all the children have had a go, try to match the right comment with the sentence. Are there any that could be OK for several sentences? Agree as a group which one goes with which.

- When they have finished, ask them 'what do you think a good comment means?'

- Ideas that the children will hopefully come up with are:
  - It needs to be a relevant comment
  - Sometimes we can just use noises or words like 'oh'
  - Questions should be relevant to what the person has just said
  - They should show that we understand how they are feeling.

- Repeat the activity with the right comment cards and ask the children to then follow their comment with a relevant question. You may choose to print out the additional cards with the prompt or you could just use the original cards and a picture of a question mark.

Variation

- Every child has a comment card. One person reads a sentence and the child who thinks their comment is suitable, stands up and then reads it out.

See CD for all relevant activity pages

Activity 9: Good commenting... sentences

> The other day I was walking through the park and this dog ran up to me and bit my leg – it really hurt

> I am very happy because next week I am going on holiday with my family

> I was wondering if it is OK to ask my friend to help me with some work – I am really struggling with it and I know she could help

> I was watching a really interesting programme last night on the television – it was all about Africa

> I am feeling very low today – my cat died at the weekend and I am very upset about it

> When I went shopping yesterday, I saw a lovely coat that I think I am going to buy

Activity 9: Good commenting... comment cards

Oh no! Poor you!	**How exciting!**
Yes I should think so	**Oh how interesting!**
I'm so sorry	**Oh!**

Activity 10: Face to face

Preparation

Print out the topics for discussion.

Laminate the cards if you wish to use them again.

Instructions

- This is the same as activity 8 (back to back) except this time they are going to practise their good listening. Ask the children to get into pairs and to choose who is going to be the speaker and who is going to be the listener.

- Explain that they are going to spend 1 minute listening to their partner and showing them they are interested by using good listening skills. Go through the different topics and explain that they can either choose one of these topics or a topic of their own.

- You may choose to do this one pair at a time with the other children observing or to do it in groups of 3 with 1 child observing the 2 talking and listening.

- Explain that you are going to rate everyone's listening on the 4 aspects of good listening using the rating chart
  - Good looking
  - Good faces
  - Good bodies
  - Good comments.

- Continue the activity until everyone has had a turn at being the listener and speaker.

- You could video the pairs and watch it back if that was appropriate for the group.

Activity 10: Face to face

You are going to tell your partner all about a nice day you have had recently

You are going to tell your partner all about something that has worried or upset you recently

You are going to tell your partner all about your favourite game or hobby and why you like it

You are going to tell your partner all about a day at school and what you liked or didn't like about it

You are going to tell your partner all about your family and who you are closest to

You are going to tell your partner all about your best friend and why you like them

Topic 4: Talkabout beginnings

Objectives:

To introduce the skills involved in 'good beginnings'

To understand the importance of starting a conversation appropriately

To help the children improve their skills in starting up a conversation

Materials:

You will need the Gary and Brad puppets

You will need to print out and copy a number of the activities

Some of the activities can be enlarged to A3

Some of the activities are best laminated so that you can use them again

Timing:

This topic will take up to 4 sessions to complete.

Topic 4: Talkabout beginnings

Activity	Teacher notes
Beginnings for Brad (Activity 11)	An activity to introduce the idea of good beginnings. Brad wants to talk to Gary and the children try to think of things he could say to get the conversation started. Introduce the 5 main ways to start a conversation: say hello, ask a question, request something, compliment or comment on the environment.
Starting out (Activity 12)	The group discuss the different ways to start a conversation and think of examples using the different categories. They could then complete the worksheet as a group or as individuals.
Pass the greeting (Activity 13)	An activity to practise good conversation starters. The children choose one of the examples and go around the group starting a conversation with someone. The other person then responds appropriately.
Musical starters (Activity 14)	An activity to further practise their skills. The children are divided into 2 groups. One group walk around the other group and when the group leader says 'stop' the children in the first group have to start a conversation with the person that is nearest to them.

 **Activity 11: Beginnings for Brad**

Preparation

You will need the Gary and Brad puppets.

Print out a number of speech bubbles to write ideas in. These can be enlarged to A3 if necessary and laminated if you wish to use non permanent markers.

Instructions

- Re-introduce Brad and Gary. Explain that Brad really wants to talk to Gary but he needs some ideas of how to start the conversation.

- Pass Brad around the group and each child tries to think of something Brad could say to start the conversation. The person holding Gary then responds.

- When everyone has had a turn, write the ideas down for starting a conversation in the speech bubbles.

- You could talk about the 5 main ways to start a conversation and divide the examples into the following:
    - General greetings, e.g. 'hi, hello'
    - Asking a question, e.g. 'where's the..?'
    - Requesting something, e.g. 'please...'
    - Complimenting, e.g. 'I like...'
    - Commenting on the environment, e.g. 'Nice day...'

 Activity 12: Starting out

Preparation

Print out the speech bubbles and the worksheets (optional).

Enlarge the speech bubbles to A3 if you are going to work as a group.

Laminate if you want to use markers.

Instructions

- Ask the children to think about each category and to come up with ideas within each one.

- Write these ideas down in the speech bubbles.

- These can be used as a display or to remind the children in later activities of the best ways to start a conversation.

- The children could then complete a worksheet (optional) with their favourite beginnings.

👤 Activity 13: Pass the greeting

Preparation

Print out and laminate the cards.

Instructions

- Ask the children to take it in turns to choose someone in the group to start a conversation with.

- They then choose a card.

- The child then starts the conversation and the other child responds.

- Continue around the group until everyone has had a turn.

- The children discuss how it went. Which ones were really good? Did any not work so well? Why?

Variation

The cards could be made into a dice (using a square box of tissues for example). The children then roll the dice to choose the conversation starter.

Activity 13: Pass the greeting

Ask a question

Say hello...

Ask for something

Comment on the weather...

Say something nice

?...

You choose

 **Activity 14: Musical starters**

Preparation

None

Instructions

- Divide the children into 2 groups. The groups need to be the same size so you may need to use one of the group facilitators if you have an odd number of children.

- One group stands in a tight circle facing outwards and the other group walk around the circle until the group leader calls 'stop'. They should then be facing one of the children in the inner circle.

- While the children are walking around the circle, the group leader tells them how they are to start the next conversation, for example, with a compliment, or a question. They may need to make it easier by telling them to start their conversation with the words 'I like…' or 'Did you know…?' or 'Please…'

- When the leader calls 'stop', the children in the outer circle start a conversation with one of the children in the inner circle using the direction from the leader. The other child then responds.

- Continue until all kinds of beginnings have been tried. Then change the circles so that the roles are reversed.

Topic 5: Talkabout taking turns

Objectives: To introduce the skills involved in 'good turn taking'

To understand the importance of taking turns in a conversation

To help the children improve their skills in turn taking

Materials: You will need the Gary and Brad puppets

You will need to print out and copy a number of the activities

Some of the activities can be enlarged to A3

Some of the activities are best laminated so that you can use them again

You may want to use your laminated mat and a bean bag for one of the activities

Timing: This topic will take up to 4 sessions to complete.

 **Topic 5: Talkabout taking turns**

Activity	Teacher notes
Gary and Brad want to talk (Activity 15)	An activity to introduce the idea of good turn taking. Gary and Brad want to get to know each other. They start the conversation off and then don't know what to do. The children think of different things that they could say. The important aspects of maintaining a conversation are highlighted: asking and answering questions, telling someone something relevant and interesting, saying something nice, taking turns to speak, listening and looking.
Getting to know Gary / Brad (Activity 16)	An activity for the children to take it in turns to be Brad and to say something to Gary using some cards as a prompt. This can be done with a bean bag and mat as in previous activities. Roles are then reversed and Gary gets to know Brad using different prompts.
Pass the buck (Activity 17)	An activity to practise good turn taking. The children take it in turns to have a conversation with the group leader using an object (the 'buck') that it passed between them. They are only allowed to talk when they are holding the 'buck'. The children then pair up and try it between themselves.
Twenty questions (Activity 18)	An activity to further practise asking questions. The children take it in turns to pick a card and the group have to guess what or who is on their card using 'yes/no' questions. Can they guess it in twenty questions? This would work well as a group cohesion activity at the end of one of the sessions.

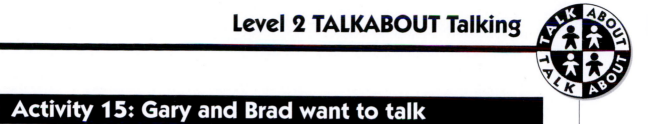

Activity 15: Gary and Brad want to talk

Preparation

You will need the Gary and Brad puppets.

Print out a number of speech bubbles to write ideas in. These can be enlarged to A3 if necessary and laminated if you wish to use non permanent markers.

Print out the Talkabout Rules for turn taking.

Instructions

- Re-introduce Brad and Gary. Explain that Gary and Brad really want to get to know each other but they need some ideas of what to say. They know how to start the conversation but what should they say then?

Gary	Hello Brad
Brad	Hello Gary
Gary	ummm
Brad	errrr
Gary	Bye Brad
Brad	Bye Gary

- Ask the children to come up with some ideas, e.g. 'how are you today?' and then write down 'ask a question'. Try to elicit the main areas of:
  - Asking questions
  - Answering questions
  - Tell them something about you that is interesting
  - Say something relevant
  - Say something nice.

- You could then model Brad getting it wrong by asking lots of questions and speaking too much and not letting Gary say anything. This will introduce the importance of taking turns.

139

Our GOOD TURN TAKING rules

1.  **Asking questions**

2. **Answering questions**

3.  **Say something relevant!**

4. Say something nice

5.  **Take turns and listen!**

Activity 16: Getting to know Gary

Preparation

You will need the Gary and Brad puppets.

Print out the prompt cards and laminate if you want to use them again. You may choose to enlarge them and stick them to your laminated mat that you have previously made for earlier activities. You will then need a bean bag.

Instructions

- Ask one child to hold Gary and to sit in the centre of the circle.

- The other children then take it in turns to hold Brad and to say something to him.

- Use the cards as prompts. These can be placed in the centre of the circle and chosen at random or could be placed on a mat in the middle of the circle. The children then throw the beanbag to choose the question / statement.

- The child holding Gary should be encouraged to respond appropriately to Brad's comment / question.

- After a few turns, the child holding Gary should change places with another child, so half of the children in the group get to be Gary.

- Explain that now Gary wants to get to know Brad. Place Brad in the centre and change the prompt cards. The children who did not get a turn to be Gary in the centre should take it in turns to be Brad in the centre.

- Continue until everyone has had a turn and all the prompt questions and comments have been used.

- How did it go?

141

Activity 16: Getting to know Gary

Find out what Gary likes to eat

Ask Gary where he lives

What is Gary's favourite hobby?

Find out if Gary has any brothers or sisters

Activity 17: Pass the buck

Preparation

You will need an object that is the 'buck'. This could be a microphone or bean bag or anything that the children can easily hold.

Instructions

- Explain that in this game you are only allowed to speak when you are holding the 'buck'.

- Explain that they are going to take it in turns to have a conversation with one of the group leaders.

- Ask one child to volunteer to have the first conversation.

- Pass the buck between the child and the leader until you have had a short conversation.

- Continue until everyone has had a turn.

- Ask the children to pair up and try it themselves. You will need extra 'bucks' for this part if the children are going to do it simultaneously.

- How did it go?

Variation

- You could bring people that the children don't know well into the session and ask the children to get to know them.

 **Activity 18: Twenty questions**

Preparation

Print out the cards or use objects / people familiar to the children in your group.

You could prepare and use a number board. You will then need a counter to move along the numbers.

Instructions

- Explain that in this game you are trying to find out what is written on a piece of card by only asking yes / no questions.

- One child starts in the 'hot seat' and selects a card.

- The rest of the children try to guess the word by using 20 questions.

- If you are using a number board, move the counter along the numbers to help the children see how they are doing.

- Encourage the children to start with general questions such as 'is it a person?' or 'is it an animal?' or 'is it an object?' You could simplify the activity by allowing the child in the hot seat to say what category the word is in first.

- Continue until every child has had a turn.

- How did it go?

Variation

- You could have a bag of objects instead of words that the child selects.

- You could make up a head band with Velcro on the front and place a card on the child's head. They then have to ask questions to find out what they are.

144

The Queen

Spider

Pencil

My teacher

Lion

Football

Level 2 TALKABOUT Talking

Topic 6: Talkabout endings

Objectives: To introduce the skills involved in 'good endings'

To understand the importance of ending a conversation appropriately

To help the children improve their skills in ending a conversation

To create a story about good conversational skills

Materials: You will need the Gary and Brad puppets

You will need to print out and copy a number of the activities

Some of the activities can be enlarged to A3

Some of the activities are best laminated so that you can use them again

Timing: This topic will take up to 5 sessions to complete.

Topic 6: Talkabout endings

Activity	Teacher notes
Gary needs to go (Activity 19)	This activity will introduce the children to the topic of how to end a conversation. Brad is talking to Gary but Gary needs to go. The children talk about what Gary could say to Brad and how Brad might know that Gary wants the conversation to end. Ideas are written down as prompts for the next activity.
Ending it with Brad (Activity 20)	An activity for the children to take it in turns to be Gary and to end the conversation using the ideas from the previous activity as prompts. Brad is initially held by the group leader who talks to the child holding Gary. Gary then tries to end the conversation. The activity continues until all the children have had a turn.
A story about conversations (Activity 21)	Use the template to help the children complete a story about why having a good conversation is important.
Talk this way (Activity 22)	The children walk around the room and practise their good conversation skills.
Certificates of achievement (Activity 23)	The children receive a certificate to celebrate their achievement. This could be their laminated record of achievement if this has been used throughout the sessions or the other general certificate for completing the level.

☃ Activity 19: Gary needs to go

Preparation

You will need the Gary and Brad puppets.

Print out a number of speech bubbles to write ideas in. These can be enlarged to A3 if necessary and laminated if you wish to use non permanent markers.

Print out the Talkabout Rules for good endings.

Instructions

- Re-introduce Brad and Gary. Explain that Gary and Brad have been having a really good conversation thanks to the children's help but now Gary needs to go. Brad is still keen to talk…

Brad   And then the next day, I was so tired. I should really have gone to bed a bit earlier but you know what it's like when you get into a game and…

Gary   (looking away, fidgeting).

- What could Gary do or say? Write the ideas down on the speech bubbles to be used in the next activity.

- If someone wants to end a conversation, what might we notice? What do you think Brad notices about Gary? Write these ideas down in the eyes.

- Go through the ideas on the Talkabout poster.

Our GOOD ENDINGS rules

1. 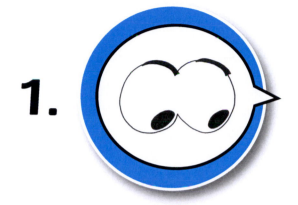 **Look away a little**

2. **Wait for a pause**

3. **Bring the conversation to an end**

4.  **Say goodbye!**

149

Activity 20: Ending it with Brad

Preparation

You will need the Gary and Brad puppets.

You will also need the completed speech bubbles from the previous activity.

Instructions

- Explain that you are going to take it in turns to be Gary and to end the conversation with Brad.

- Brad is held by one of the group leaders and Gary is given to one of the children. The speech bubbles with the prompts should be placed in the centre of the circle for ideas.

- Brad then starts talking to Gary and the child holding Gary should try and wait for a pause and then end the conversation.

- The person holding Brad should respond appropriately to Gary's endings.

- How did it go?

- Continue until everyone has had a turn at ending the conversation and all the prompt questions and comments have been used.

- Were there some endings that worked better than others?

- Take it in turns to be Brad as well as Gary.

Activity 21: A story about conversations

Preparation

Choose whether you want to use colour or black and white. Print out the story template.

You may also want to collect some pictures or photographs to illustrate the story, for example, of a child listening or 2 people talking.

You will also need scissors, glue and possibly colouring pens.

When the story is finished, you will need to laminate it or put it in plastic wallets to keep safe.

Instructions

- Tell the children you are going to write a story about having a good conversation. When they have written it, you are going to make it into a book to read.

Suggestions for the story

- Page 1 'A story about having conversations. Talking to people is very important. This story is about good conversations.'
  - Illustrate using photos of the children or pictures of people talking

- Page 2 'Talking to people is good. I like to talk to…'
  - Suggestions: … my friends; my family; my teachers…
  - Illustrate with pictures of friends, family etc or people talking

- Page 3 'When I talk to people, I try to use good speaking. This is important because…'
  - Suggestions: … people will understand what I am saying; they will want to talk to me; it is polite to use a good voice…
  - Illustrate with someone speaking

Activity 21: A story about conversations

Suggestions for the story continued

- Page 4 'When I talk to people I try to use good listening. I can show people I am listening to them by...'
  - Suggestions: ... looking at them; using a good face; making comments
  - Illustrate with a photo of someone listening

- Page 5 'When I start a conversation, I could say...'
  - Suggestions: ... hello there; nice day; I like your...; where's the bus?
  - Illustrate with a photo of someone starting a conversation

- Page 6 'I could keep the conversation going by doing good turn taking. This means I might...'
  - Suggestions:... ask them questions; tell them something interesting; say something nice; listen to them...
  - Illustrate with photos of the children talking to each other

- Page 7 'I could end the conversation by saying...'
  - Suggestions: ... well I must be going now; it's been good talking to you...
  - Illustrate with someone saying or waving goodbye

- Page 8 'I will try to do good talking and listening when I am having a conversation. My .... will be happy. My .... will be happy'
  - Suggestions: ... mum, teacher, friends, family
  - Illustrate with lots of people looking happy.

See CD for all relevant activity pages

Activity 22: Talk this way

Preparation

Print out *Our Talkabout Talking Rules* (activity 2) to use as a prompt.

Instructions

- Recap on the rules and put them somewhere in the room where everyone can see them.

- Ask the children to walk around the room and when the group leader calls 'STOP', the children have to pair up and have a conversation with each other.

- The children use the rules to help them remember what they need to do.

- How did it go?

- You could then ask someone to come into the group and the children could practise their skills in having a conversation with someone different.

Activity 23: Certificates of achievement

Preparation

Print out the certificates and laminate if possible.

Instructions

- Give the children their certificate with a round of applause!

Contents

		C/V*	Page

*C/V = colour version of worksheet available on the CD

Introduction

Aim of this level	To increase awareness into assertiveness skills and to improve skills in using effective body language and speaking skills when being assertive.
Topics covered	1. Saying something 2. Saying what I think 3. Saying how I feel 4. Saying no 5. Saying sorry 6. Saying something nice!
Materials	A number of the activities throughout this level use animals so I do try and find puppets or soft toys to play the key roles. Animals that are useful are owl, lion, mouse, worm, snake, frog, ape, newt, dog and cat.
Length of level	This level will take up to 20 lessons depending on the ability of the students and the length of the lessons.
Students	Groups work best if the children get on and are well matched for both personality and need. Aim for a group of between 4 and 8 people. Remember that a larger group will mean the level may take longer to complete.
Group gelling	Factors that can help group cohesion are: group cohesion activities (see pages 247–48); get the group to decide on a name for the group; devise some group rules; make sure everyone takes part; and good leadership.
Format of the sessions	1. Group cohesion activity 2. Recap 3. Main activity(s) 4. Group cohesion activity.
Confidentiality	Remind everyone that the content of the sessions is not to be discussed with other students outside of the session.

156

👤 Topic 1: Saying something

Objectives: To introduce assertiveness

To gel the group

To introduce the importance of saying things assertively as opposed to saying things passively or aggressively. The skills of saying what you think, how you feel, apologising, refusing and complimenting are also introduced

Materials: You may choose to get 3 animals to help with the characters in the story: a mouse, an owl and a lion

You will need to print out and copy a number of the activities

Some of the activities are best enlarged to A3

Some of the activities are best laminated so that you can use them again

You will need Velcro for one activity

Timing: This topic will take up to 5 sessions to complete.

Topic 1: Saying something

Activity	Teacher notes
The lion, the mouse and the owl (Activity 1)	*A story that introduces the children to 3 animals who are passive, aggressive and assertive. The children have to help the animals make their way back to the circus by deciding who has the best ideas.*
We're on our way to the circus (Activity 2)	*An active game where the children progress around the room based on the instructions on the cards (similar to snakes and ladders).*
The assertive scale (Activity 3)	*The children consider behaviours that could be described as passive, aggressive or assertive. They then complete a worksheet.*
Being a wise owl (Activity 4)	*A poster is prepared for the children to refer to for the rest of the level.*

Activity 1: The lion, the mouse and the owl

Preparation

You may wish to use 3 soft toys – a lion, a mouse and an owl. Alternatively you can just use the pictures of the 3 animals.

Print out the story and the pictures.

Print out the story board if you are going to use it.

You may wish to enlarge this to A3.

Laminate the story and pictures if you wish to use them again.

Instructions

- You may want to use 3 facilitators: one to play the Lion, one to play the Mouse and one to play the Owl.

- Explain to the children that they are going to listen to a story.

- They are going to help the animals get back home to the circus by choosing what they should do.

- When you go through the story, the children can either just choose which option is best or they may like to place the right picture in the story board.

- Alternatively, they can do this as a second activity after the story.

- You can then talk about:

  1. Can the children identify why the Owl was wise?

  2. Do they ever feel like the Lion or the Mouse?

  3. Why is it better to be like the Owl?

- The children could then complete the worksheet 'The Wise Owl...' using the pictures from the story to think about what a wise Owl does.

See CD for all relevant activity pages

Activity 1: The lion, the mouse and the owl

The Lion, the Mouse and the Owl

 Activity 1: The lion, the mouse and the owl

Chapter 1
The circus has left town

It's early in the morning and the circus has left town. They left in the middle of the night, moving their caravans out of the clearing in the wood and slowly driving on to the next town.

Suddenly there is a loud noise. Who is that waking up in the clearing? Oh no, it's Roaring Richard the Lion.

Lion   (Shouting) WHERE IS EVERYONE? I'M HUNGRY!

The Lion is furious! He has obviously been left behind by the circus! But wait a minute… someone else is waking up – it's Timid Timothy the Mouse.

Mouse   (Whispering) Hello? Where is everyone? I'm frightened!

The Mouse is frightened and doesn't like being away from the other mice at the circus. He is starting to panic when Wise William the Owl says…

Owl   Don't worry Timothy. Don't worry Richard. It appears that the 3 of us have been left behind. We must talk about what we should do.

Activity 1: The lion, the mouse and the owl

Three animals lost in the wood.
What shall they do?

Lion   (Shouting) Well I think we should SHOUT and run around lots – someone will hear us and will come to rescue us.

Mouse   (Whispering) I think we should curl up and hide – they will find us sooner or later.

Owl   I think we should keep calm and search for clues to see which way the caravans went.

Can you help? What do you think they should do?

Activity 1: The lion, the mouse and the owl

Chapter 2
The animals set off on their journey

Of course Wise William was right and so the animals searched for clues in the clearing of the wood.

Suddenly Timid Timothy found some tracks. The tracks were heading straight into a dark and scary forest.

Owl   We have to follow the tracks into the forest. They will lead us to the circus. And if we hurry we will be there before lunch.

But the Lion, the Mouse and the Owl all looked into the dark forest and stopped. They were scared. What should they do?

Activity 1: The lion, the mouse and the owl

Three animals scared in the forest.
What shall they do?

Lion   (Shouting) It will make us feel better if we shout lots and hit anything that gets in our way!

Mouse   (Sniffing) Oh no... I think we should stay here, very quietly and cry a little.

Owl   Oh no... I think we should talk about how we are feeling and help each other to be brave. We can do it if we stick together.

Can you help? What do you think they should do?

Activity 1: The lion, the mouse and the owl

Chapter 3
The animals go into the forest

Of course Wise William was right. Talking about how they felt made them feel a bit better. They agreed to be brave and set off on their journey.

The forest was very dark and it was sometimes difficult to see where they were going. They were bumping into trees and bumping into bushes! Suddenly, they bumped straight into a group of Rabbits who were sleeping. The Rabbits were not very happy! They were tired and grumpy as they had been up all night.

Oh dear... a group of unhappy Rabbits. What should they do?

Owl   We must all say sorry for disturbing the Rabbits.

165

Activity 1: The lion, the mouse and the owl

Three animals saying sorry.
Which one is best? The Lion goes first.

Lion   (Shouting) SORRY! But you were in my way and we are in a hurry!

Mouse   (Quietly) Sorry, sorry, sorry, sorry, sorry, sorry

Owl   I am sorry to have woken you. Please excuse us – we were in such a hurry and didn't see you.

Can you help? Which one do you think is best?

166

Activity 1: The lion, the mouse and the owl

Chapter 4
The animals meet a friendly fox

Of course Wise William was right and the Rabbits felt happier and said goodbye and good luck.

The Lion, the Mouse and the Owl set off again. It was now the middle of the day and they were determined to get to the circus before tea time. They knew they were all expected to be in tonight's performance and they didn't want to miss it.

They were feeling happier and stopped to have a quick drink from a stream. Suddenly a very friendly Fox approached them and said hello. He was very interested in their story and wanted to help them follow the tracks. Foxes are very good at that! They liked the Fox. His name was Felix.

After a while, the Fox told them about a party he was going to that evening. Everyone was going to be there and Felix wanted his new friends to come too. He said that he was sure the circus could manage without the Lion, the Mouse and the Owl for one night.

Oh *dear*... what should they do? Wise William said:

Owl   We must all say no to the Fox.

Activity 1: The lion, the mouse and the owl

Three animals saying no to the Fox.
Which one is best? The Lion went first.

Lion   (Shouting) NO DON'T BE SILLY! We can't come with you.

Mouse   (Quietly) Oh dear... I don't think we can come. I'm not sure.
               What do you think?

Owl   I am sorry but we can't come. It is important that we get back
              to the circus.

Can you help? Which one do you think is best?

Activity 1: The lion, the mouse and the owl

Chapter 5
The animals meet a policeman

Of course Wise William was right. They had to refuse the Fox's kind invitation but they said goodbye and wished him a happy evening.

The Lion, the Mouse and the Owl set off again. They had been travelling now for many hours and were getting hungry. Suddenly they came to a crossroads. They searched for clues but couldn't see any tracks.

Oh dear... three lost animals and the day is nearly over. They saw a policeman nearby – maybe he could help them? What should they do?

Owl   We should ask the policeman if he knows where the circus is in town. He might be able to show us the way to go.

But the Lion and the Mouse looked worried. They were not sure that the Owl was right. What should they do?

169

Activity 1: The lion, the mouse and the owl

Three animals lost at the crossroads.
What shall they do?

Lion   (Loudly) Oh don't bother asking him, he won't know – FOLLOW ME, I'm always right!

Mouse   (Quietly) Oh yes, we can't speak to the policeman – we won't know what to say. I think we should just follow the Lion.

Owl   I think we should ask him. We should ask him if he can help us find our way to the circus.

Can you help? What do you think they should do?

170

Activity 1: The lion, the mouse and the owl

Chapter 6
The animals make it to the circus

Of course Wise William was right. The policeman was very helpful and showed them the right way to go.

The Lion, the Mouse and the Owl set off again. They had now been travelling all day and they were tired and hungry. Suddenly they saw bright lights ahead of them. They looked at each other in excitement. There was the circus and there were all their friends!

Oh hurray…

Owl   Well thank goodness we are home!

Lion   WE'RE BACK! WE'RE HERE! WE'RE HUNGRY!

Mouse   Hello, hello, hello!

Activity 1: The lion, the mouse and the owl

The other animals were amazed to see them and wanted to hear all about their adventure.

Lion   Well we had to SHOUT to frighten lots of people and fierce animals away and we had to fight to survive!

Really? Everyone said.

Mouse   No! We just had to keep calm, tell each other how we were feeling and be brave and ask for help from a policeman. Oh, and we also had to say sorry to some Rabbits and say no to a Fox!

Lion   Actually, all we had to do really was to listen to Wise William – he always had the right idea! Clever Owl!

The End

Activity 2: We're on our way to the circus

Preparation

You will need to print out and make up the cards. You may like to back the cards with the pictures. You will need to copy this page x 4.

You will also need 20 chairs lined up around the room with a start position and a finish position. It is easiest to place them in a 'snake' fashion so that the line bends round on itself several times. To make the game shorter, use fewer chairs.

This activity does not work well with large groups of children. I play it with no more than 6.

You may like to get masks or give the children an animal to be during the game. They could then make their animal noise when it is their turn.

Instructions

- Explain to the children that they are all going to try to make it to the circus. It is a game that is similar to snakes and ladders but the chairs are going to be the places on the board and the children will actually move around the 'board' themselves.
- All the children stand at the start of the line and explain that the circus is at the end of the line.
- All the cards are placed in a pile or in a bag.
- The first child takes a card (or is read a card) and follows the instructions.
- The game continues until all children have reached the end of the line (the circus).
- You may want to have a list of the children on the board in the order they are playing so that everyone knows whose turn it is next.
- The children could then discuss what they learnt and what kinds of behaviour got the best results.

173

 Activity 2: We're on our way to the circus

Activity 2: We're on our way to the circus

Well done!
You have listened to Wise William and you are being very friendly. Move forward 6 places and say 'hello' to everyone you pass

Oh dear! The Lion has tried to eat one of the clowns but he thought it tasted funny!!
Go back 2 places!

Oh dear! Timid Timothy has hidden in the bushes again. You spend 1 hour trying to find him.
Stay where you are!

Oh good! Wise William has said sorry to the Rabbits and we can now move on.
Go forward 4 places

Oh dear! The Lion has scared the Rabbits and made them cry. He must stop shouting!
Go back 1 place!

Oh dear! The Mouse is too frightened to ask the policeman for help and so you are still lost.
Stay where you are!

👤 Activity 3: The assertive scale

Preparation

You will need to print out and make up the rating scale and cards. The rating scale is best laminated with a Velcro strip along the bottom so that cards can be placed along the scale. Velcro will then need to be attached to the back of the cards.

Photocopy the pictures and worksheets if the children are going to complete these.

Instructions

- Introduce the rating scale to the children.

- Explain that sometimes people behave a bit like the Mouse and can be described as 'passive'. Sometimes they behave like the Lion and can be described as 'aggressive' and sometimes they behave like the Owl and can be described as 'assertive'.

- Ask the children to take it in turns to pick up a card and to think about the description. Do they think that describes the Mouse, Lion or Owl? They then place the card along the rating scale.

- The activity continues until all the cards have been used.

- Can the children think of any other behaviour that the Mouse, Lion or Owl might use?

- They can then complete the worksheets if they want to. Give each child a copy of all the pictures and 3 worksheets. Ask them to work in pairs to work out what the Lion would be like, and cut and stick the appropriate pictures onto their worksheets.

See CD for all relevant activity pages

The Assertiveness Scale...

Passive

Assertive

Aggressive

1 . . . . 2 . . . . 3 . . . . 4 5

This page may be photocopied for instructional use only. *Talkabout for Children* © Alex Kelly 2011

Speechmark

Activity 4: Being a wise owl

Preparation

Choose whether you want to use colour or black and white and print out the rules. You may also choose to enlarge the card.

You will want to laminate it so that it can be referred to every week.

Instructions

- Introduce the Wise Owl sheet. Explain that these are the areas that they are going to be thinking about for the next few sessions and that they can use this poster to help them every week.

- Saying what we think

- Saying how we feel

- Saying no

- Saying sorry

- Saying something nice – complimenting others.

 # Being a Wise Owl

We will try to...

1.  **Say what we think**

2. **Say how we feel**

3.  **Say no**

4. **Say sorry**

5.  **Say something nice**

Topic 2: Saying what I think

Objectives: To introduce the importance of saying what you think assertively as opposed to saying what you think passively or aggressively

To understand the importance of STOP, THINK, SPEAK & LISTEN

To help the children improve their skills

Materials: You will need a number of objects and soft toys to encourage the children to make up a story

You will need to print out and copy a number of the activities

Some of the activities are best enlarged to A3

Some of the activities are best laminated so that you can use them again

Timing: This topic will take up to 2 sessions to complete.

Topic 2: Saying what I think

Activity	Teacher notes
Tell me a story (Activity 5)	The children are asked to make a story up as a group involving a number of objects and soft toys. They work as a small group to create their story and share it with the others.
Stop, think, speak & listen (Activity 6)	The children are introduced to the 4 key prompt cards to being assertive. What does it mean for each one when you want to say what you think?

 Activity 5: Tell me a story

Preparation

You will need a number of objects and soft toys that will encourage the children's imagination. Alternatively you can just use pictures or both.

I may use: a teddy, a couple of soft animals, a mobile phone, a bandage, a ball, some keys, a car, a picture of a river, a picture of the moon, a book, some sweets and a bottle of drink.

This activity works best in small groups of between 3 and 6 children. You may need to divide the group into 2 groups. You will therefore need 2 sets of objects – either the same or different.

You will also need to print out the pictures and worksheets (optional).

Instructions

- Explain to the children that they are going to make up a story by looking at all the objects and pictures they have been given and involving all of them in a story.

- The small group of children sit around the circle with the objects and give their ideas. They need to be supported by a facilitator who writes the story on a large piece of paper.

- The children can then tell or act out their story to the other children (or to themselves) by using the objects and pictures as props.

- Ask the children what they needed to do to tell the others in the group their ideas.

- The children then use the cards to consider which ones are good and which ones are not good when telling people what we think. They may want to complete the worksheet.

See CD for all relevant activity pages

 Activity 6: Stop, think, speak & listen

Preparation

You will need to print out and laminate the prompt cards and / or poster.

Print out the worksheets (optional).

Instructions

- Introduce the 4 prompt cards to the children – what do they think they mean?

- Why are they important?

- Alternatively you can use the poster to help the children think about the 4 steps to being assertive.

- The children can then complete the worksheet by adding in their ideas:

  1. STOP, e.g. wait for a pause, put up my hand
  2. THINK, e.g. what am I going to say?
  3. SPEAK, e.g. say it nicely, speak clearly, use a good face and body
  4. LISTEN, e.g. look at the person, use a good face and body.

See CD for all relevant activity pages

 Activity 6: Stop, think, speak & listen

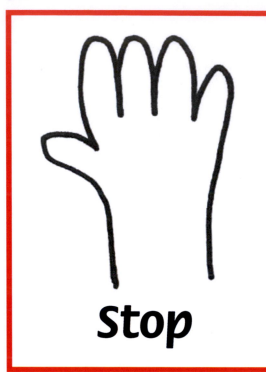

Stop

Think

Speak

Listen

Topic 3: Saying how I feel

Objectives: To introduce the importance of saying how you feel in an assertive manner

To help the children improve their skills

Materials: You may choose to get some animals to help with the characters in the story: a worm, an ape, a snake, a newt and a frog

You will need to print out and copy the stories

These activities are best laminated so that you can use them again

Timing: This topic will take up to 7 sessions to complete.

Topic 3: Saying how I feel

Activity	Teacher notes
Funny feelings at the circus (Activity 7)	Introduce the children to 5 animals at the circus who are struggling with their feelings. Over the next few sessions, the children have to help the animals by deciding what they should do.
Feeling worried (Activity 8)	Wilma the worm is worried about her headaches. Wilma asks her friends for advice and the children decide which animal she should listen to. Can the children think of times they have been worried. Who could they talk to and what could they say? The children practice 'I feel… because…'
Feeling nervous (Activity 9)	Natty the newt is nervous about the high wire. She asks her friends for advice. Can the children think of times when they have been nervous? The children practice 'I feel… because…'
Feeling angry (Activity 10)	Arthur the ape is angry because Roger the rat has been telling the other animals lies about him. He asks his friends for their advice and the children decide who has the best idea. Can the children think of times they have felt angry. The children practice 'I feel… because…'
Feeling frightened (Activity 11)	Frankie the frog is frightened because he has to sleep on his own tonight. He asks his friends for advice and the children decide who has the best idea. Can the children think of times they have been frightened? The children practice 'I feel… because…'
Feeling sad (Activity 12)	Sammy the snake is sad because his friend Sally has moved to another circus. He asks his friends for advice and the children decide who has the best idea. Can the children think of times they have been sad? The children practice 'I feel… because…'
Saying how I feel rules (Activity 13)	A poster to encourage the children to remember the rules for saying how they feel.

Activity 7: Funny feelings at the circus

Preparation

Print out all the stories and worksheets.

Laminate the stories if you wish to reuse.

Instructions

- Explain to the children that sometimes we have feelings that are difficult to cope with and we need to learn to tell people how we feel.

- Show the children the 5 characters in the stories

- Story 1: Wilma the worm is worried

- Story 2: Natty the newt is nervous

- Story 3: Arthur the ape is angry

- Story 4: Frankie the frog is frightened

- Story 5: Sammy the snake is sad.

Activity 7: Funny feelings at the circus

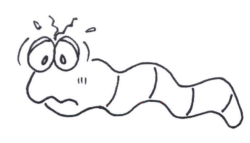

Funny Feelings
at the circus

Five stories about feelings

👤 Activity 8: Feeling worried

Preparation

Print out the story and worksheet.

Laminate the story if you wish to reuse.

Instructions

- Explain to the children that they are going to listen to a story.

- Read the first page of the story and ask the children to think about the suggestions made by the friends. Who has the best idea?

- Then ask the children what they think Wilma should say to the doctor.

- Ask the children to think of times they have been worried. Add these ideas to page 3 (or just talk about them). The children think of who they could talk to and what they could say.

- Introduce them to the 'I feel… because…' way to express our feelings assertively. The separate worksheet is optional. Introduce the rules for saying how we feel.

Activity 8: Feeling worried

Wilma the worm
is worried

Activity 8: Feeling worried

Wilma the worm is worried

Wilma the worm is a very popular and friendly worm. She is normally very happy and healthy. But today she is not very happy.

Wilma the worm has woken up with another headache. She has had a headache for several weeks and she is now feeling very worried. In fact, she is so worried that she is actually feeling a little sick.

She decides to ask her friends for their advice.

Sheila the sheep thinks she should stop worrying and take another pill.

Pete the parrot thinks she should take a long nap and see how she feels tomorrow.

Ollie the otter thinks she should go to the doctor and tell him she is worried.

 Activity 8: Feeling worried

Who is right? Which friend should she listen to?

Wilma the worm decides to listen to Ollie the otter and goes to the doctor to tell him she is worried.

What do you think she should say?

Wilma says 'Hello doctor. I am very worried about my headaches. I have been having them for several weeks and I think something is wrong with me. I am feeling rather worried'.

The doctor looks at Wilma. He talks to Wilma. He asks Wilma lots of questions. And then he does some tests on Wilma.

And do you know what is wrong? Wilma is getting headaches because she needs glasses! Poor Wilma – all that worrying!

Wilma the worm is now not worried. She is enjoying her new glasses! What a lot of things she can see now!

Activity 8: Feeling worried

Feeling worried...

Sometimes we feel worried.
What do you worry about?

_____

_____

Who could you talk to?

_____

_____

What could you say?
Try saying...

'I feel... _____

because... _____

_____ ,

Wilma the worm will be very pleased that we are telling someone how we are feeling!

 Activity 9: Feeling nervous

Preparation

Print out the story and worksheet.

Laminate the story if you wish to reuse.

Instructions

- Explain to the children that they are going to listen to a story.

- Read the first page of the story and ask the children to think about the suggestions made by the friends. Who has the best idea?

- Then ask the children what Natty should do.

- Ask the children to think of times they have been nervous. Add these ideas to page 3 (or just talk about them). The children think of who they could talk to and what they could say.

- The separate worksheet is optional.

Activity 9: Feeling nervous

Natty the newt is nervous

Activity 9: Feeling nervous

Natty the newt is nervous

Natty the newt is a brave and happy newt. She has only been with the circus for a few months but she loves it and has made lots of friends. But today she is not very happy.

Natty the newt is nervous. She is so nervous that she found it difficult to sleep last night and she didn't eat much for breakfast either. Natty the newt definitely has a funny feeling in her tummy.

The circus master has asked Natty to run along the high wire tonight. He says she will be great at it. Natty the newt has never been so nervous! She doesn't know what to do.

She decides to ask her friends for their advice.

Douglas the dog thinks she should go and talk to the circus master and tell him how she's feeling.

Harry the horse thinks she should keep quiet and just do it!

Petra the panda thinks she should pretend she is ill and then she won't have to do it.

 Activity 9: Feeling nervous

Who is right? Which friend should she listen to?

Natty the newt decides to listen to Douglas the dog and goes off to find the circus master to tell him how she is feeling.

What do you think she should say?

Natty says 'Hello circus master. I need to talk to you. I am feeling very nervous about tonight and I don't know what to do about it.'

The circus master is very kind. He listens to Natty and thinks about what Natty is saying. He is impressed that Natty has come to talk to him in such a grown up way. He suggests that Natty might feel happier if she has a few more days to practise before doing it in front of the big crowds.

Natty the newt is not feeling so nervous anymore. She feels better for talking to the circus master and she is happy that she will have a few more days to practise. She is even feeling a little excited now!

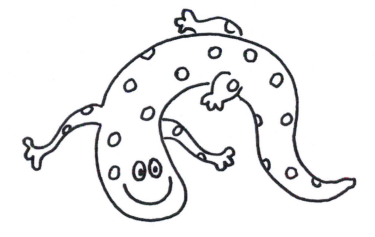

197

👤 Activity 9: Feeling nervous

Feeling nervous...

Sometimes we feel nervous.

What do you feel nervous about?

_____

_____

 Who could you talk to?

_____

_____

 What could you say?
Try saying...

'I feel... _____

because... _____

_____ '

 Natty the newt will be very pleased that we are telling someone how we are feeling!

Activity 10: Feeling angry

Preparation

Print out the story and worksheet.

Laminate the story if you wish to reuse.

Instructions

- Explain to the children that they are going to listen to a story.

- Read the first page of the story and ask the children to think about the suggestions made by the friends. Who has the best idea?

- Then ask the children what Arthur should do.

- Ask the children to think of times they have been angry. Add these ideas to page 3 (or just talk about them). The children think of who they could talk to and what they could say.

- The separate worksheet is optional.

See CD for all relevant activity pages

🏃 Activity 10: Feeling angry

Arthur the ape
is angry

Activity 10: Feeling angry

Arthur the ape is angry

Arthur the ape is a lovely chap. He is chatty and cheerful. He is cuddly and calm. But today he is not very happy.

Arthur the ape is angry. He is so angry that he thinks he is actually furious. He has found out that Roger the rat has been saying some very nasty things about him to his friends in the circus. Arthur the ape has never been so angry before and he doesn't like it! And he doesn't know what to do.

He decides to ask his friends for their advice.

George the giraffe says he should step on Roger's tail and not let him go until he has squealed for 10 minutes and said sorry 10 times!

Clara the cat thinks he should tell Roger that he is angry and talk about it to him.

Felicity the Flamingo thinks he should start telling stories about Roger the rat! That would show him!

 Activity 10: Feeling angry

Who is right? Which friend should he listen to?

Arthur the ape decides to listen to the cat and tell Roger how he is feeling.

What do you think he should say?

Arthur says 'Hello Roger. I need to talk to you. I am angry because I have heard the lies you have been telling my friends. I would like you to stop and to say sorry for doing this'.

Roger the rat looks at Arthur. He listens to Arthur and then thinks about what Arthur is saying. He is impressed that Arthur has talked to him in such a grown up way. He decides that Arthur is right and he says sorry to him.

Arthur the ape is not angry anymore. He feels better for talking to Roger the rat and he is happy that they have sorted out their problems. He is back to his old cuddly, calm, chatty and cheerful self!

Activity 10: Feeling angry

Feeling angry...

Sometimes we feel angry.

What do you feel angry about?

_____

_____

Who could you talk to?

_____

_____

What could you say?
Try saying...

'I feel... _____

because... _____

_____ '

Arthur the ape will be very pleased that we are telling someone how we are feeling!

Activity 11: Feeling frightened

Preparation

Print out the story and worksheet.

Laminate the story if you wish to reuse.

Instructions

- Explain to the children that they are going to listen to a story.

- Read the first page of the story and ask the children to think about the suggestions made by the friends. Who has the best idea?

- Then ask the children what Frankie should do.

- Ask the children to think of times they have been frightened. Add these ideas to page 3 (or just talk about them). The children think of who they could talk to and what they could say.

- The separate worksheet is optional.

Activity 11: Feeling frightened

Frankie the frog is frightened

Activity 11: Feeling frightened

Frankie the frog is frightened

Frankie the frog is a very funny frog. He is always making people laugh with his funny faces and his funny jokes. But today he is not very happy.

Frankie the frog is frightened. He is so frightened that he can't stop shaking. He has been at the circus for many years now and has always shared a room with a friend or two. But tonight he has got to sleep alone. The circus master has decided to give him a room all to himself. Frankie the frog has never slept alone. He is feeling very frightened indeed. And he doesn't know what to do.

He decides to ask his friends for their advice.

Marty the monkey says he is sure he will be fine as soon as he falls asleep.

Fergus the fly says he should go and talk to the circus master and tell him how he's feeling.

Boris the bear says he should not say anything to anyone and then sneak into his room – he would look after him.

(☆) Activity 11: Feeling frightened

Who is right? Which friend should he listen to?

Frankie thinks that Boris the bear is very kind to offer to share his room but decides to listen to Fergus the fly and goes off to find the circus master to tell him how he is feeling.

What do you think he should say?

Frankie says 'Hello circus master. I need to talk to you. I am feeling very frightened about tonight. I don't like the idea of sleeping alone and I don't know what to do about it'.

The circus master is very kind. He listens to Frankie and thinks about what Frankie is saying. He is impressed that Frankie has come to talk to him in such a grown up way. He says that Frankie doesn't have to have a room on his own and he is very happy for him to return to sharing with his friends.

Frankie the frog is so relieved and is not feeling frightened anymore. He feels better for talking to the circus master and is happy that he can share with his friends. Frankie is back to being a funny frog!

207

Activity 11: Feeling frightened

Feeling frightened...

Sometimes we feel frightened.
What do you feel frightened about?

_____

_____

Who could you talk to?

_____

_____

What could you say?
Try saying...

'I feel... _____

because... _____

                                              ,

_____

Frankie the frog will be very pleased that we are telling someone how we are feeling!

⚐ Activity 12: Feeling sad

Preparation

Print out the story and worksheet.

Laminate the story if you wish to reuse.

Instructions

- Explain to the children that they are going to listen to a story.

- Read the first page of the story and ask the children to think about the suggestions made by the friends. Who has the best idea?

- Then ask the children what Sammy should do.

- Ask the children to think of times they have been sad. Add these ideas to page 3 (or just talk about them). The children think of who they could talk to and what they could say.

- The separate worksheet is optional.

Activity 12: Feeling sad

Sammy the snake is sad

Activity 12: Feeling sad

Sammy the snake is sad

Sammy the snake is always smiling. He is a happy, smiley kind of snake who is always happy to help. But today he is not very happy.

Sammy the snake is sad. He is so sad that he can't stop crying. His best friend, Sally has just left the circus to join another one. They have been best friends for several years and Sammy misses her so much. He is feeling very sad. And he doesn't know what to do.

He decides to ask his friends for their advice.

Rupert the rabbit suggests that he gets himself a pet. This might make him feel happier.

Wally the walrus says that Sammy should run away and try and find the other circus.

Elsie the elephant says they should all gather round and make Sammy feel better. They should spend some time with him – he needs to know he still has friends.

211

Activity 12: Feeling sad

Who is right? Which friend should he listen to?

Sammy thinks that Elsie the elephant is very kind to offer to spend some time with him and they sit down and have a good talk about how he is feeling.

What do you think he should say?

Sammy says 'I feel very sad. I miss my friend Sally so much.'

Elsie the elephant is very kind. She listens to Sammy and then makes him feel better by inviting all his other friends around to spend some time with them both.

Sammy the snake starts to feel better. He still misses his friend Sally, but talking to Elsie and his other friends makes him feel better. He is happy that he has such good friends. He even manages a few smiles!

Activity 12: Feeling sad

Feeling sad...

Sometimes we feel sad.

What do you feel sad about?

_____

_____

Who could you talk to?

_____

_____

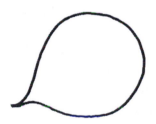

What could you say?
Try saying...

'I feel... _____

because... _____

                                                  ,

_____

Sammy the snake will be very pleased that we are telling someone how we are feeling!

 Activity 13: Saying how I feel

Preparation

Choose whether you want to use colour or black and white and print out the rules. You may also choose to enlarge the card.

You may want to laminate it so that it can be referred to every week.

Instructions

- Ask the children to recap on what is important when you are telling people how you feel.

- **Think before you speak**

- **Say 'I feel... because...'**

- **Speak clearly**

- **Use a good face and body**

- **Listen to the other person.**

- Can the children think of any other feelings that are difficult to express? Can they think of examples?

- If they can, spend some time role playing these and practising 'I feel... because...' using the rules.

saying how I feel

Remember to...

1.  **Think before you speak**

2. **Say 'I feel...**
because...'

3.  **Speak clearly**

4. **Use a good face**
and body

5.  **Listen to the other**
person

Topic 4: Saying no

Topic 4

Objectives: To introduce the importance of saying no in an assertive manner

To help the children improve their skills

Materials: You may choose to get a toy dog to help with the story

You will need to print out the story and the rules

These activities are best laminated so that you can use them again

Timing: This topic will take up to 3 sessions to complete.

Topic 4: Saying no

Activity	Teacher notes
Douglas the dog learns to say no (Activity 14)	The children listen to a story about Douglas the dog who is learning to say no. The children help come up with ideas for how he should say no to the rabbits, cat, rat and a stranger and finally to the circus master.
Saying no (Activity 15)	A poster to encourage the children to remember the rules for saying no. The children then practise these using role play.

 Activity 14: Douglas the dog learns to say no

Preparation

Print out the story and laminate if you wish to reuse.

You will also need a marker pen to add in the children's ideas.

Instructions

- Explain to the children that they are going to listen to a story about Douglas the dog who finds it difficult to say no. They are going to help Douglas by thinking of how he can say no.

- Add in the best way to say 'no' on each page.

- Ask the children to think about times they have had to say no.

- What is important to remember?

Douglas the dog learns to say no

A story about a dog saying 'no'

Activity 14: Douglas the dog learns to say no

Douglas says no to the rabbits

Douglas the dog is a very friendly dog. He likes nothing more than making people happy. The trouble is he finds it difficult to say no.

Today he has an important job to do for the circus master. He has been asked to go to the shop to buy some sweets for tonight's performance. Douglas has to hurry otherwise the children won't have any sweets and the circus master will be cross.

He is running out of the gate when he meets his friends the rabbits.

Rupert the rabbit says 'come and play with us Douglas'.

Oh no... Douglas knows he has to say no but he doesn't know how to do it nicely.

Can you help? What should Douglas say?

_____

_____

Thank you! The rabbits are fine about Douglas saying no and say they will play with him later.

Activity 14: Douglas the dog learns to say no

Douglas says no to a cat

Douglas the dog is pleased with himself for not getting distracted by the rabbits' game and he continues on to the shop.

He is now on his way through the wood when suddenly he hears Clara the cat calling to him. Where is she? Oh poor Clara – she is stuck up a tree and can't get down.

Clara explains that she was being chased by her friend Katie when she got stuck up the tree. Katie has gone to get George the giraffe who will help Clara get down but Clara wonders if Douglas would be very kind and stay and talk to her for 10 minutes while they wait for George.

Oh no. Douglas knows he has to say no but he feels sorry for Clara and wants to say it very nicely. Can you help? What should Douglas say?

_____

_____

Thank you! Clara the cat completely understands and says she will be fine and she will see him on his way back.

Activity 14: Douglas the dog learns to say no

Douglas says no to a rat

Douglas the dog is pleased with himself for being able to say no to Clara and he continues on to the shop. He is making good progress.

Suddenly he comes across Roger the rat who seems to be having fun throwing sticks into the river and chasing after them. Roger wants Douglas to join in his game.

Douglas remembers he has to say no, so he says 'No thank you Roger, I can't today. I am going to the shop for the circus master and I need to hurry'. Douglas is pleased with himself – he knows he has said no nicely. But Roger doesn't seem to listen to him.

Roger says 'oh come on Douglas. Don't be boring. Come and play with me for 5 minutes. You can make up the time by running fast'.

Oh no. Douglas knows he has to say no a bit more firmly. Can you help? What should Douglas say?

_____

_____

Thank you! Roger the rat listens to him this time and says they will play the game another day.

222

Activity 14: Douglas the dog learns to say no

Douglas says no to a stranger

Douglas the dog is pleased with himself for being able to say no to Roger and he continues on to the shop. He is nearly there now.

Douglas comes to a road. He stops and looks both ways before crossing. He is pleased to stop for a minute as he is very tired from all that running.

Suddenly a car stops. The man looks very friendly and asks Douglas if he is OK. Douglas knows he mustn't talk to strangers, so he just says 'yes thank you' and goes to carry on. But the man wants to give him a lift and says 'You look tired. Let me give you a lift up the road. I am sure I am going your way.'

Oh no. Douglas is a bit frightened. He knows he has to say no in a very clear and strong way. Can you help? What should Douglas say?

_____

_____

Thank you! The man drives off and Douglas continues onto the shop. Phew!

223

Activity 14: Douglas the dog learns to say no

Douglas says no to the circus master

Douglas the dog is proud of himself. He reaches the shop in very quick time and buys the sweets that the circus master wants. Now all he has to do is run all the way back to the circus.

On the way he checks to see if Clara is OK. Luckily George has arrived so she is happy now. He waves at Roger and then at the rabbits and then he runs up to the circus master.

The circus master is very happy with Douglas and asks if his journey went well. Douglas says he has learnt to say 'no' in lots of different ways and he now understands that sometimes you need to say no very nicely and sometimes you have to say no more firmly and sometimes you have to be very strong and just say 'NO'.

The circus master is very pleased and asks Douglas if he would like to go for a walk with him before the show starts.

Oh no. Douglas is so tired after all that running and doesn't think he can manage a walk! But he remembers what he has learnt and says 'no thank you, I am afraid I am a little tired.'

The circus master is very understanding and is happy that Douglas has learnt to say no. Phew! thinks Douglas. Time for a rest!

Activity 15: Saying no

Preparation

Choose whether you want to use colour or black and white and print out the rules. You may also choose to enlarge the card.

You may want to laminate it so that it can be referred to again.

Instructions

- Ask the children to recap on what is important when you are saying no.

- Show the children the Saying No rules.

- Can the children think of times they have had to say no?

- If they can, spend some time role playing these and practising saying no assertively using the rules to help them.

Saying No

Remember to...

1.  **Think about *how* you need to say no**

2. **You may need to say...**

- **NO!**
- **No thank you**
- **No I am sorry I can't because...**

3.  **Speak clearly**

4. **Use a good face and body**

Speechmark

Topic 5: Saying sorry

Objectives: To introduce the importance of saying sorry in an assertive manner

To help the children improve their skills

Materials: You will need to print out the cards and the rules

These activities are best laminated so that you can use them again

You will also need 2 facilitators to model the behaviours in the first activity

Timing: This topic will take up to 3 sessions to complete.

👤 Topic 5: Saying sorry

Activity	Teacher notes
Say sorry! (Activity 16)	The children watch a series of role plays to illustrate poor apologising and good apologising. Can they see which are the good ones and which ones are not so good?
The lion & mouse learn to say sorry (Activity 17)	An activity to encourage the children to think about how to say sorry in different situations using scenarios from the circus.
Saying sorry (Activity 18)	A poster to encourage the children to remember the rules for saying sorry. Can they think of times they have had to say sorry? How did it go? The children then practise using role play.

Activity 16: Say sorry!

Preparation

Print out the 'good' and 'bad' cards in Activity 5 'Tell me a story' – one for each child.

You will also need 2 facilitators to model the behaviours.

You may need a marker pen to write down the children's ideas.

Instructions

- Explain to the children that they are going to watch the facilitators do some acting and the children are going to decide whether they were good or bad at saying sorry.

- Choose a scenario that is easy to model. An ideal one is both seated across from one another talking and one of the facilitators kicks the other one in the shin while crossing their legs.

  1. In the first scenario, the person does not apologise at all, even though the other person says 'Ow!' They just pause and then carry on talking

  2. In the second scenario they apologise but say it insincerely and then carry on

  3. In the third scenario they say it nicely but then keep on doing it (each time say it nicely) so they don't seem to learn

  4. In the fourth scenario they say it nicely but don't take responsibility for it and blame the other person (e.g. 'move your leg and then it won't happen again')

  5. In the fifth scenario, they over apologise and embarrass the other person

  6. In the final one they apologise appropriately.

- After each scenario, ask the children to hold up their good or bad cards and then say what was bad about it.

 Activity 17: The lion & mouse learn to say sorry

Preparation

Print out the cards and laminate if you want to use them again.

You may want to back them with the pictures of the animals

Print out the worksheets if you are going to use them.

Instructions

- Explain to the children that they are going to help Roaring Richard and Timid Timothy to say sorry nicely.

- The children take it in turns to pick a card. They discuss the story and then choose a second person to play the other character.

- They then try to say sorry nicely and the other character responds.

- If the children are uncomfortable doing the role play, the children could direct the facilitators to do it for them.

- Continue until all the children have had a turn and all the stories have been discussed.

- Complete the worksheet (optional).

Activity 17: The lion & mouse learn to say sorry

Activity 17: The lion & mouse learn to say sorry

Oh dear, Roaring Richard has stepped on Roger the rat's tail and Roger is now in a lot of pain.

Can you show Richard how to say sorry to Roger?

Oh dear, Timid Timothy has frightened Elsie the elephant and Elsie is now looking very pale and standing on a stool.

Can you show Timothy how to say sorry to Elsie?

Oh dear, Roaring Richard was practising his scary roar and has woken up Rupert the rabbit. Rupert is now very grumpy.

Can you show the lion how to say sorry to Rupert?

Oh dear, Timid Timothy has eaten the last of the cheese and there is nothing for Roger the rat to eat for tea. Roger is hungry and grumpy.

Can you show Timothy how to say sorry to Roger the rat?

 Activity 18: Saying sorry

Preparation

Choose whether you want to use colour or black and white and print out the rules. You may also choose to enlarge the card.

You may want to laminate it so that it can be referred to again.

Instructions

- Ask the children to recap on what is important when you are saying sorry.

- Go through the rules.

- The group then discuss if they had to say sorry recently.

- What did they do? What did they say? How did it go? Do they think they should have done something differently?

- Can they practise saying sorry assertively using the rules to help them?

saying Sorry

Remember to...

1. Think *about how* you need to say sorry

2. You will need to say sorry...

- ...and mean it!
- ...and sometimes give a reason

3. Say it nicely

4. Use a good face and body

234

Topic 6: Saying something nice

Objectives: To introduce the importance of paying compliments.

To help the children improve their skills.

Materials: You may choose to get a toy cat to help with the story

You will need to print out the story and the rules

These activities are best laminated so that you can use them again.

Timing: This topic will take up to 4 sessions to complete.

Topic 6: Saying something nice

Activity	Teacher notes
Clara the complimenting cat (Activity 19)	The children listen to a story about Clara the cat who is learning to pay compliments. The children help come up with ideas for how she could do it better. They then try to give compliments to each other.
Saying something nice (Activity 20)	A poster to encourage the children to remember the rules for saying something nice. They can then practise these using role plays and games.
Certificates of achievement (Activity 21)	The children receive a certificate of achievement and a round of applause!

Activity 19: Clara the complimenting cat

Preparation

Print out the story and laminate if you wish to reuse.

Print out the worksheet if you are going to use it.

Instructions

- Explain to the children that they are going to listen to a story about Clara the cat who wants to learn how to pay a compliment. They are going to help Clara by thinking of how she can do it well.

- Ask the children to think about a time when someone has said something nice to them. How did it make them feel?

- What is important to remember when we are saying something nice?

  1. Smile
  2. Use a nice voice
  3. Say something that is true.

Activity 19: Clara the complimenting cat

Clara
the complimenting cat

A story about saying something nice

Activity 19: Clara the complimenting cat

Clara the cat is complimented

Clara the cat is having a very happy day. The sun is shining and it is fish for tea. She is very excited.

Clara is also happy because her friend Douglas the dog has just said something very nice to her. He told her that her fur is looking very shiny today and it makes her look very pretty. She is so pleased and says 'thank you so much Douglas!' Now Clara can't stop smiling and singing to herself.

Clara decides that she wants to make the other animals in the circus happy too so she rushes off to find someone to compliment.

239

Activity 19: Clara the complimenting cat

Clara compliments Boris the bear

Clara rushes off to find someone to compliment.

Suddenly she sees Boris the bear. She is very excited and rushes over to him with the compliment.

Hello Boris, she says. Your fur is looking very shiny today – it makes you look very pretty. But Boris doesn't look very happy. He scowls at Clara and tells her to go away. He seems to be upset that she called him 'pretty'.

Oh dear. What went wrong? The compliment didn't work with Boris. It seemed to make him cross. Can you think of anything to help Clara?

Clara wonders if she should try another compliment but Boris has already gone. So she goes off in search of someone else.

Clara compliments George the giraffe

Clara looks around and sees George the giraffe in the field. She is determined to get it right this time so she rushes up to George.

George is wearing a lovely new scarf so Clara thinks she will say something nice about it. But she wants George to hear her compliment, so she stands on a fence and shouts up at him.

HELLO GEORGE, she shouts. I LIKE YOUR SCARF!

George jumps a little and chokes on the leaf he is chewing. He hadn't seen Clara there and now he is coughing and going very red. Oh thank you Clara, he manages to say. But he doesn't look very happy. He still looks a bit jumpy and worried.

Oh dear. What went wrong? The compliment didn't seem to work with George either. Can you think of anything to help Clara?

But Clara doesn't want to give up and she thinks she should try another compliment. So she goes off in search of someone else.

Activity 19: Clara the complimenting cat

Clara compliments Sammy the snake

Clara leaves the field and heads back to the circus. On the way she meets Sammy the snake. She thinks about complimenting Sammy but to be honest, Sammy makes her feel a bit nervous. Clara has never found it easy to be around the snakes, even though Sammy is a very friendly snake.

But Clara is determined to make everyone as happy as she is. So she takes a deep breath and says,

Hello Sammy. You look very nice today. Is that a new hat?

But Sammy looks at Clara in a rather suspicious way. Clara was being very serious and she looked rather nervous. So he thinks she doesn't mean it and slithers off into the grass without saying another word.

Oh dear. What went wrong this time? The compliment didn't seem to work with Sammy either and she really tried hard this time. Can you think of anything to help Clara?

Clara decides to ask her friend Douglas the dog for some help.

Activity 19: Clara the complimenting cat

Clara talks to Douglas

Clara rushes off to find Douglas the dog. Surely he will be able to tell her what she is doing wrong.

Douglas the dog is very helpful. Clara explains that she gave Boris the bear the same compliment as Douglas had given her but Boris didn't like it. Douglas laughs and says that compliments only work if they are true and not just repeated. Boris knew she didn't mean it, because he certainly isn't pretty!

Clara then tells him about George and Sammy. Douglas thinks that she shouldn't have shouted the compliment to George and she should have smiled at Sammy when she gave him the compliment.

Clara thinks Douglas is very clever. Who else would know all the rules behind saying something nice to others?

Clara smiles at Douglas. You are clever, she says. And you are such a good friend!

Douglas smiles again. Thank you for the compliment! He says. I think you have learnt how to compliment others very nicely!

Clara is so happy and rushes off to find Boris, George and Sammy. She is sure she will get it right this time!

243

Activity 20: Saying something nice

Preparation

Choose whether you want to use colour or black and white and print out the rules. You may also choose to enlarge the card.

You may want to laminate it so that it can be referred to again.

Instructions

- Ask the children to recap on what is important when you are saying something nice.

- Go through the rules.

- Has anyone had a nice compliment recently? What was said?

- Can they practise complimenting each other using the rules to help them?

- They may like to take turns to leave the room while everyone else thinks about suitable compliments to give that person. The leader could then write these down. When the child enters the room, the list is read out to them. Alternatively the children give their compliments one by one. How did it make them feel?

saying something nice

Remember to...

1.  **Think about *what* you are going to say...**

2. **Say something real or genuine (the truth)**

3.  **Use a nice voice**

4. **And smile!**

Activity 21: Certificates of achievement

Preparation

Print out the certificates and laminate if possible.

Instructions

- Give the children their certificate with a round of applause!

Contents

 Introduction

Aim of this section

Group cohesion activities are an essential part of any group.

They are needed at the beginning of any period of intervention to help the group gel.

They are then needed at the beginning of subsequent sessions to ease the children into the group and to help everyone feel involved.

They are also needed at the end of the session to reduce any stress and to help children leave the group feeling happy.

It is helpful for a lot of children to have this familiar routine to a group:
- Group cohesion activity
- Main activity(s)
- Group cohesion activity.

The best group cohesion activities are easy, fun and involve everyone.

On the CD you will find 25 of my favourite group cohesion activities.

See CD for all relevant activity pages

Contents

Introduction   The following section is a suggested plan of intervention following two academic years. Only the main activity is suggested for each session.

Every session   Every session should include:
- A group cohesion activity of your choice
- The main activity
- A group cohesion activity of your choice.

In addition, I also do a 'How are you feeling?' activity after the first group cohesion game and a 'How did you do?' activity at the end. Formats for these can be found in the first TALKABOUT for Children book – developing self awareness and self esteem.

Terms 1 & 2   Aims to improve the child's body language.

Terms 3 & 4   Aims to improve the child's conversational skills.

Terms 5 & 6   Aims to improve the child's assertiveness skills.

Timing   The intervention plan is based on 6 terms of 12-13 weeks and a 40–45 minute session, although progress will depend on the age and ability of the children as well as the length of session and size of group.

TALKABOUT for CHILDREN

Term 1 BODY LANGUAGE term 1

TOPIC: Talking body language & talking faces

Week	Main Activity	Equipment / preparation	Your notes
	Every week	Group cohesion activity of your choice How do I feel? (optional) **Main activity** How did I do? (optional) *Group game*	• How do I feel board (every week) • How did I do poster (every week) • Props for group cohesion activities • Props for main activity(s)	
1	Group rules Group cohesion activities	• Props for group cohesion activities	
2	Activity 1 silent movies	• silent movies cards printed out and laminated • Prompts for group leaders (optional) • A camera	
3	Activity 2 Building bodies	• Print out and enlarge the body and body parts • Colour in the body parts and laminate • A feely bag • Building bodies worksheet (optional)	
4	Activity 3 Dissecting bodies	• Print out worksheets and enlarge if possible • Photos from activity 1 or photos of different emotions • Scissors and glue	
5	Activity 4 Talking body parts Activity 5 Our TALKABOUT rules	• Print out talking body part cards and laminate • Print out and laminate TALKABOUT rules	

250

Term 1 BODY LANGUAGE term 1

TOPIC: Talking body language & talking faces

Week	Main Activity	Equipment / preparation	Your notes
6	Activity 6 The blindfold game	• A blindfold for everyone • Print out discussion cards	
7	Activity 7 Find a face	• A number of faces showing different emotions • Print out the brainstorm and enlarge to A3 • Scissors and glue	
8	Activity 8 Bingo faces	• Print out and prepare bingo boards and cards • Counters or stickers to cover up bingo pictures	
9	Activity 9 Making masks	• Print out and prepare masks on card • Lolly sticks (or an equivalent)	
10	Activity 10 Emotional sentences	• Print out sentences • Masks from the previous week	
11	Activity 11 Why are faces important?	• Print out worksheets and cards	
12	Activity 12 A story about faces	• Print out story template • Photos from activity 1 and/or faces from magazines / internet etc • Scissors, glue and colouring pens (optional)	
13	Certificates of achievement ceremony	• Laminated certificates	

TALKABOUT for CHILDREN

Term 2 BODY LANGUAGE term 2

🏃 TOPIC: Talking faces, talking bodies & talking space

Week	Main Activity	Equipment / preparation	Your notes
Every week	Group cohesion activity of your choice How do I feel? (optional) Main activity How did I do? (optional) Group game	• How do I feel board (every week) • How did I do poster (every week) • Props for group cohesion activities • Props for main activity(s)	
1	Read the story about faces Activity 13 Stop and stare	• A story about faces laminated • Props for group cohesion activities	
2	Activity 14 A day in the life	• Print out sentences and story board for a day in the life • Glue (optional)	
3	Activity 15 Walk this way! Activity 16 Posture thermometer	• A camera • Print out thermometer and enlarge if possible • Photos of different emotions or emotion cards from activity 8 • Worksheets, scissors and glue (optional)	
4	Activity 17 When we are tense / relaxed	• Print out worksheets and enlarge if possible • Print out pictures • Scissors and glue	
5	Activity 18 Why are bodies important?	• Print out worksheets and cards • Scissors and glue	

TALKABOUT for CHILDREN

Term 2 BODY LANGUAGE term 2

TOPIC: Talking faces, talking bodies & talking space

Week	Main Activity	Equipment / preparation	Your notes
6	Activity 19 A story about our bodies	• Print out story template • Photos from activity 15 and/or faces from magazines / internet etc • Scissors, glue and colouring pens (optional)	
7	Activity 20 Give us a hand	• Print out cards • A very large piece of paper or 4 pieces of flip chart paper stuck together	
8	Activity 21 Space control	• Print out worksheets (optional) • A camera (optional)	
9	Activity 22 Touch control	• Print out the 2 sets of cards and laminate or place on the sides of tissue boxes to create 2 dice • Worksheets, scissors and glue	
10	Activity 23 What happens when…	• Print out worksheets and emotions • Scissors and glue	
11	Activity 24 A story about space	• Print out story template • Photos from activity 21 and/or pictures of people from magazines / internet etc • Scissors, glue and colouring pens (optional)	
12	Activity 25 Space hoppers	• Print out 'touch' cards from activity 22 and 2 additional ones. Enlarge if possible. • Print out situation cards	
13	Activity 26 Certificate of achievement ceremony	• Laminated certificates	

Term 3 CONVERSATION SKILLS term 1

TOPIC: Talkabout talking, talkabout speaking & talkabout listening

Week	Main Activity	Equipment / preparation	Your notes
Every week	Group cohesion activity of your choice How do I feel? (optional) **Main activity** How did I do? (optional)	• How do I feel board (every week) • How did I do poster (every week) • Props for group cohesion activities • Props for main activity(s)	
1	Group game Group rules Group cohesion activities	• Props for group cohesion activities	
2	Activity 1 A puppet show	• 2 puppets to be 'Gary' and 'Brad' • Print out scripts and 'good' and 'bad' cards • Print out cards for the rules	
3	Activity 1 A puppet show continued Activity 2 Our Talkabout rules	• 2 puppets to be 'Gary' and 'Brad' • Print out scripts and 'good' and 'bad' cards • Print out cards for the rules • Print out and laminate the rules	
4	Activity 3 Talking to Gary	• Gary and Brad puppets • Good speaking card from Activity 1 • Print out and laminate speaking and topic cards	
5	Activity 4 Turn up the volume	• Print out and make up the rating scale using Velcro along the bottom • Print out cards and laminate and use Velcro on the back	

TALKABOUT for CHILDREN

Term 3 CONVERSATION SKILLS term 1

★ TOPIC: Talkabout talking, talkabout speaking & talkabout listening

Week	Main Activity	Equipment / preparation	Your notes
6	Activity 5 Racing rates	• Print out and make up the rating scale using Velcro along the bottom • Print out cards and laminate and use Velcro on the back	
7	Activity 6 Why is good speaking important?	• Print out worksheets and enlarge if possible • Print out cards • Scissors and glue	
8	Activity 7 Gary and Brad have a chat	• Gary and Brad puppets • Print out the 6 scenarios	
9	Activity 8 Back to back	• Print out topic cards • 2 chairs back to back • Print out and laminate the good listening rules	
10	Activity 9 Good commenting	• Print out sentences and comment cards	
11	Activity 10 Face to face	• Print out topics for discussion and rating chart	
12	Activity 11 Beginnings for Brad	• Gary and Brad puppets • Print out speech bubbles and enlarge to A3 if possible • A large marker pen	
13	Certificates of achievement ceremony	• Laminated certificates	

Term 4 CONVERSATION SKILLS term 2

TOPIC: Talkabout beginnings, talkabout taking turns and talkabout endings

Week	Main Activity	Equipment / preparation	Your notes
Every week	Group cohesion activity of your choice How do I feel? (optional) **Main activity** How did I do? (optional) Group game	• How do I feel board (every week) • How did I do poster (every week) • Props for group cohesion activities • Props for main activity(s)	
1	Recap on group rules Recap on activity 11 Group cohesion activities	• Props for group cohesion activities • Speech bubbles from activity 11	
2	Activity 12 Starting out	• Print out speech bubbles and enlarge to A3 if possible • Print out worksheets (optional) • Marker pen	
3	Activity 13 Pass the greeting	• Print out cards	
4	Activity 14 Musical starters	• None	
5	Activity 15 Gary and Brad want to talk	• Gary and Brad puppets • Print out speech bubbles and enlarge if possible • Print out turn taking rules	

TALKABOUT for CHILDREN

Term 4 CONVERSATION SKILLS term 2

TOPIC: Talkabout beginnings, talkabout taking turns and talkabout endings

Week	Main Activity	Equipment / preparation	Your notes
6	Activity 16 Getting to know Gary / Brad	• Gary and Brad puppets • Print out prompt cards • A bean bag (optional)	
7	Activity 17 Pass the buck	• An object that is the 'buck', e.g. a bean bag, microphone, stick	
8	Activity 18 Twenty questions	• Print out the cards • Or use objects or photos of familiar people • A number board (optional)	
9	Activity 19 Gary needs to go	• Gary and Brad puppets • Print out speech bubbles and enlarge if possible • Print out rules for good endings	
10	Activity 20 Ending it with Brad	• Gary and Brad puppets • Speech bubbles from previous activity	
11	Activity 21 A story about conversations	• Print out the story template • Pictures and photos to illustrate the story • Scissors and glue	
12	Activity 22 Talk this way	• The TALKABOUT Talking rules from activity 2	
13	Activity 23 Certificates of achievement ceremony	• Laminated certificates	

TALKABOUT for CHILDREN

Term 5 ASSERTIVENESS term 1

TOPIC: Saying something, saying what I think & saying how I feel

Week	Main Activity	Equipment / preparation	Your notes
Every week	Group cohesion activity of your choice How do I feel? (optional) **Main activity** How did I do? (optional) Group game	• How do I feel board (every week) • How did I do poster (every week) • Props for group cohesion activities • Props for main activity(s)	
1	Group rules Group cohesion activities	• Props for group cohesion activities	
2	Activity 1 The lion, the mouse and the owl	• 3 soft toys – a lion, mouse and owl (optional) • Print out pictures of animals and story • Print out storyboard and pictures	
3	Activity 1 The lion, the mouse and the owl continued	• As previous session • Worksheets (optional)	
4	Activity 2 We're on our way to the circus	• Print out and laminate cards • 20 (or thereabouts) chairs lined up in the room • Animal masks (optional) • Print out and make up the rating scale using Velcro along the bottom	
5	Activity 3 The assertive scale	• Print out cards and laminate and use Velcro on the back • Photocopy pictures and worksheets	

TALKABOUT for CHILDREN

Term 5 ASSERTIVENESS term 1

TOPIC: Saying something, saying what I think & saying how I feel

Week	Main Activity	Equipment / preparation	Your notes
6	Activity 3 The assertive scale continued Activity 4 Being a wise owl	• As previous session • Print out and laminate the Wise Owl rules	
7	Activity 5 Tell me a story	• A number of objects and pictures to encourage the children's imagination	
8	Activity 5 Tell me a story continued Activity 6 Stop, think, speak & listen	• Print out pictures and worksheets • Print out and laminate prompt cards and assertive poster • Worksheets (optional)	
9	Activity 7 Funny feelings at the circus Activity 8 Feeling worried	• Print out story • Worksheets (optional)	
10	Activity 9 Feeling nervous	• Print out story • Worksheets (optional)	
11	Activity 10 Feeling angry	• Print out story • Worksheets (optional)	
12	Activity 11 Feeling frightened	• Print out story • Worksheets (optional)	
13	Certificates of achievement ceremony	• Laminated certificates	

TALKABOUT for CHILDREN

Term 6 ASSERTIVENESS term 2

TOPIC: Saying how I feel, saying no, saying sorry & saying something nice

Week	Main Activity	Equipment / preparation	Your notes
Every week	Group cohesion activity of your choice How do I feel? (optional) **Main activity** How did I do? (optional) Group game	• How do I feel board (every week) • How did I do poster (every week) • Props for group cohesion activities • Props for main activity(s)	
1	Recap on group rules Recap on activities 7-11 Group cohesion activities	• Props for group cohesion activities • Stories	
2	Activity 12 Feeling sad	• Print out story • Worksheets (optional)	
3	Activity 13 Saying how I feel	• Saying how I feel rules	
4	Activity 14 Douglas the dog learns to say no	• Print out story	
5	Activity 15 Saying no	• Print out and laminate the rules for saying no	

Speechmark

TALKABOUT for CHILDREN

Term 6 ASSERTIVENESS term 2

🏃 TOPIC: Saying how I feel, saying no, saying sorry & saying something nice

Week	Main Activity	Equipment / preparation	Your notes
6	Activity 16 Say sorry!	• Print out good and bad cards from activity 5	
7	Activity 17 The lion & mouse learn to say sorry	• Print out the cards and laminate • Print out worksheets (optional)	
8	Activity 18 Saying sorry	• Print out and laminate the rules for saying sorry	
9	Activity 19 Clara the complimenting cat	• Print out story • Print out worksheets (optional)	
10	Activity 20 Saying something nice	• Print out and laminate the rules for saying something nice	
11	Recap on previous work on body language and conversation skills	• Props as appropriate	
12	Recap on previous work on body language and conversation skills	• Props as appropriate	
13	Activity 21 Certificates of achievement ceremony	• Laminated certificates	

Contents | Page

Plan of intervention

GROUP —————————————— Date ————

TOPIC for term ——————————————————

Children ——————————————————

Week	Plan	Equipment	Your notes

Speechmark

👤 My Talkabout targets (1)

Child's name _____ Date _____

Overall aim _____

Intervention this term _____

TARGETS this term _____

1. _____

2. _____

3. _____

STRATEGIES to use within the classroom

1. _____

_____

2. _____

_____

3. _____

_____

Completed by _____ Date _____

🏃 My Talkabout targets (2)

My name _____ Date _____

My aim is to _____

What I will be doing _____

MY TARGETS	0 Skill not present	1 Skill emerging with prompting	2 Skill emerging with occasional prompting	3 Skill present in a structured situation	4 Skill present in some other situations	5 Skill present and consistent across most situations
1.						
2.						
3.						

How did I do? _____

Signed _____ Date _____

Speechmark Ⓢ Ⓟ

How did I do? (1)

Name _____

😀 I did well   😐 I did ok   😞 It was hard

Code:
✓✓ = achieved
✓ = skill emerging
✗ = skill not present

Date	How did I do?			Evaluation of main activity	Comments	Signed
	😀	😐	😞			

🚶 How did I do? (2)

Name _____

Date	How did I do? 🙂 🙂 🙁			One thing I'd like to say ...	Signed

Session evaluation

GROUP _____ Date _____ Session number _____

TOPIC for term _____

Children present _____

	Plan	Evaluation
Starter activity		
Main activities		
Finishing activity		

Completed by _____ Date _____

Certificate of achievement

Awarded to

_____

Congratulations!

You have successfully completed...

_____

Signed _____

Index

 Index

Index